RICHARDS MEMORIAL LIBRARY

3 1460 00076 3952

P9-CNH-886

THE WORLD'S GREATEST AIRCRAFT
CIVIL AIRCRAFT

THE WORLD'S GREATEST AIRCRAFT
CIVIL AIRCRAFT

Christopher Chant: edited by Michael J.H. Taylor

Chelsea House Publishers • Philadelphia

Published in 2000 by
Chelsea House Publishers
1974 Sproul Road, Suite 400
P.O. Box 914
Broomall. PA, 19008-0914

ISBN 0-7910-5421-7

Copyright © 2000 Regency House Publishing Limited

Photographs on pages 2, 3, 4, 5, 6–7, 8, 11, 12, 14-15,
62 courtesy Michael J.H. Taylor

All rights reserved. No part of this publication may be
reproduced, stored in a retrieval system, or transmitted in
any form or by any means, electronic, mechanical,
photocopying, recording or otherwise, without the prior
permission of the copyright holders.

Printed in China

Library of Congress Cataloging-in-Publication Data

Chant, Christopher.
      Civil aircraft / by Christopher Chant.
            p.   cm. -- (The world's greatest aircraft)
      Originally published as part of the author's: The world's
greatest aircraft. London: Grange Books, 1997.
      Includes index.
      Summary: Drawings, photographs, and text describe a
variety of civilian aircraft, both U.S. and foreign, including
the Cessna planes. Satic Beluga, Boeing 747, Vikers VC10.
and the European Airbus.
      ISBN 0-7910-5421-7 (hc.)
      1. Transport planes -- Juvenile literature. [1. Transport
planes. 2. Airplanes.] I. Title. II. Series.
TL685.4.C49 1999
629.133'34--do21
                                                   99-30414
                                                        CIP

Page 2: Lockheed Super Constellation over New York
Page 3: Saab 2000
Right: Cessna Grand Caravan
Frontispiece: McDonnell Douglas MD11

3 1460 00076 3952

Civil Piston-Engined Transports

The 'stick and string' aeroplanes that pioneered flying in the early years of the 20th century had enough difficulty keeping the pilot aloft without the added complication of a commercially viable payload. And yet, hardly had the Wright brothers recovered from the exhilaration of their first-ever powered flights than a letter arrived from a businessman, enquiring whether they could transport minerals by air over a 26-km (16-mile) hop in West Virginia, for which they would be paid $10 per ton. Politely, the offer was turned down for practical reasons.

However, a much developed Wright Model B biplane was used in November 1910 to carry the first-ever air freight, this time 542 yards of silk transported between Dayton and Columbus. The cost of the flight to the Morehouse-Martens Company was a staggering $5,000, yet the flight generated such interest in the company's Home Dry Goods Store that, by cutting some silk into small pieces for sale as souvenirs attached to postcards, Morehouse-Martens showed an overall profit from the venture of over $1,000.

This and similar high-publicity flights were little more than advertising stunts, but already in 1910 the first-ever commercial passenger airline had begun operating in Germany, carrying over 34,000 passengers without injury until November 1913. Known as Delag, the airline had been founded by Count von Zeppelin and consequently operated giant airships. At the start of the following year, in 1914, the first-ever scheduled airline services using an aeroplane (Benoist flying-boat) began in Florida, but these lasted only a few months.

Even while World War I raged at its bloodiest, British and German civil airline companies were registered for post-war activities, allowing operations to start in 1919. Progress in aeroplane development had, by then, made commercial operations viable. Very little time passed before other airlines began to appear, able to call upon cheap ex-military aircraft that could be crudely converted for their new peacetime roles, while the first purpose-designed commercial transports were but a step away.

Picture: The piston-engined Lockheed Constellation had been designed for commercial use but first served with the U.S.A.A.F. as the C-69 wartime military transport. To expand MATS post-war long-range transport capacity, Super Constellations followed as C-121s

JUNKERS F 13 (Germany)

Junkers F 13

From its DI single-seat fighter and CLI two-seat escort fighter and close-support warplane of 1918, both all-metal monoplanes that saw limited service in World War I, Junkers developed Europe's single most important transport of the 1920s, the classic F 13 low-wing monoplane with a single nose-mounted engine and fixed tail wheel landing gear. This used the metal construction patented by Dr Hugo Junkers in 1910 for thick-section cantilever monoplane wings and was the world's first all-metal purpose-designed commercial transport.

The F 13 first flew in June 1919, and was based on nine spars braced with welded duralumin tubes and covered in streamwise corrugated duralumin skinning to create an immensely strong and durable structure. The accommodation comprised an open cockpit for two pilots and an enclosed cabin for four passengers. The cockpit was later enclosed, and the engine of the first machine was a 119-kW (160-hp) Mercedes D.IIIa inline, which was superseded in early production aircraft by the 138-kW (185-hp) BMW IIIa inline that offered much superior performance. Production continued to 1932, and amounted to at least 320 and probably 350 aircraft in more than 60 variants with a host of modifications and different engines, the most frequent being the 156-kW (210-hp) Junkers L-5 inline.

The main operator of the type was Junkers Luftverkehr, which operated more than 60 aircraft in a period between 1921 and 1926, in the process flying some 15,000,000 km (9,300,000 miles) and carrying nearly 282,000 passengers. The airline then became part of Deutsche Luft-Hansa (later Deutsche Lufthansa) which still had 43 such aircraft in service in 1931. The other F 13s were used by civil and military operators in most parts of the world. The fact that the type was immensely strong, needed little maintenance, and could operate from wheel, ski or float landing gear, made the F 13 especially popular with operators in remoter areas.

The Junkers F 13 was a light but enduring light transport

JUNKERS F 13
Role: Light passenger transport
Crew/Accommodation: One, plus up to four passengers
Power Plant: One 185 hp BMW III A water-cooled inline
Dimensions: Span 14.47 m (47.74 ft) length 9.6 m (31.5 ft); wing area 39 m² (419.8 sq ft)
Weights: Empty 1,150 kg (2,535 lb); MTOW 1,650 kg (3,638 lb)
Performance: Cruise speed 140 km/h (75.5 mph) at sea level; operational ceiling 3,000 m (9.843 ft); range 725 km (450 miles)
Load: Up to 320 kg (705 lb) payload

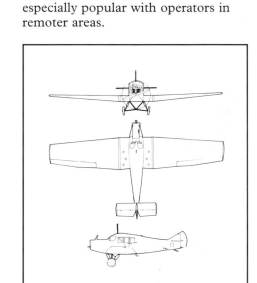

Junkers F 13

FOKKER F.VII-3m (Netherlands)

Fokker F.VIIB-3m Southern Cross, used in 1928 for the first flight across the Tasman Sea

In 1924-25, Fokker built five examples of its F.VII powered by the 268-kW (360-hp) Rolls-Royce Eagle inline engine, and then evolved the eight-passenger F.VIIA that first flew in March 1925 with a 298-kW (400-hp) Packard Liberty 12 engine and a number of aerodynamic refinements and simple three-strut rather than multi-strut main landing gear units. The type undertook a successful demonstration tour of the United States, and orders were received there and in Europe for 42 aircraft with inline or radial engines in the class between 261 and 391 kW (350 and 525 hp); licensed production was also undertaken in several countries. The type was a typical Fokker construction, with a welded steel-tube fuselage and tail unit covered in fabric, and a high-set cantilever wing of thick section and wooden construction. For the Ford Reliability Tour of the United States, Fokker produced the first F.VIIA-3m with a powerplant of three 179-kW (240-hp) Wright Whirlwind radials mounted one on the nose and the others on the main landing gear struts below the wing.

All subsequent production was of the three-engined type, and many F.VIIAs were converted. The F.VIIA-3m spanned 19.30 m (63 ft 3.75 in), but to meet the requirement of Sir Hubert Wilkins for a long-range polar exploration type, a version was produced as the F.VIIB-3m with wings spanning 21.70 m (71 ft 2.5 in). This also became a production type. Dutch construction of the two F. VII-3m models was 116 aircraft, and large numbers were built under licence in seven countries. The British and American models were the Avro Ten and Atlantic F.7. The type was also adopted by the U.S. Army Air Corps and U.S. Navy as the C-2 and RA respectively. The F.VII-3m was of great importance in the development of European and third-world transport for passengers and freight, and was also used extensively for route-proving and record-breaking flights.

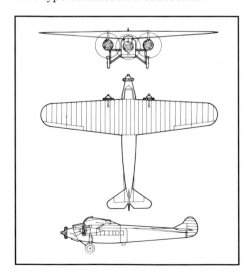

Fokker F.VIIB-3m

FOKKER F.VIIB-3m
Role: Passenger Transport
Crew/Accommodation: Two, plus up to 8 passengers
Power Plant: Three 240 hp Gnome-Rhone Titan air-cooled radials (the aircraft was equipped with various makes/powers of European and U.S. radials)
Dimensions: Span 21.70 m (71.19 ft); length 14.20 m (46.56 ft); wing area 71.20 m² (722 sq ft)
Weights: Empty 3,050 kg (6,724 lb); MTOW 5,250 kg (11,574 lb)
Performance: Maximum speed 185 km/h (115 mph) at sea level; operational ceiling 4,875 m (15,994 ft); range 837 km (520 miles) with full payload
Load: Up to 1,280 kg (2,822 lb)

Fokker F.VIIA-3m Josephine Ford, used by American Lt. Cdr. Richard Byrd for the first

FORD TRI-MOTOR (U.S.A.)

Ford 4-AT

The much loved Ford Tri-Motor was the result of Henry Ford purchasing the Stout Metal Airplane Company in 1925, which had developed the Pullman 6-passenger monoplane, and progressing on to the larger design. Remembered for its corrugated all-metal construction, it gained the nickname 'Tin Goose'. From his 2-AT Pullman powered by a single 298-kW (400-hp) Packard

Liberty inline engine, William B. Stout had evolved the 3-AT with three uncowled radial engines mounted two on the wings and one low on the nose. This was unsuccessful, but paved the way for th 4-AT that first flew in June 1926 with three 149-kW (200-hp) Wright

Whirlwind J-4 radials located two under the wings in strut-braced nacelles and one in a neat nose installation. The 4-AT accommodated two pilots in an open cockpit and eight passengers in an enclosed cabin.

The type was produced in variants that ranged from the initial 4-AT-A to the 4-AT-E with 224-kW (300-hp) Whirlwind J-6-9 radials and provision for 12 passengers. Production totalled 81 aircraft, and was complemented from 1928 by the 5-AT with 13 passengers, span increased by 1.17 m (3 ft 10 in), and three 313-kW (420-hp) Pratt and Whitney Wasp radials. Production continued up to 1932, and these 117

aircraft included variants up to the 5-AT-D with 17 passengers in a cabin given greater headroom by raising the wing 0.203 m (8 in). Other variants were four 6-ATs based on the 5-AT but with Whirlwind J-6-9 engines, one 7-AT conversion of a 6-AT with a 313-kW Wasp, one 8-AT conversion of a 5-AT with only the nose engine, one 9-AT conversion of a 4-AT with 224-kW Pratt and Whitney Wasp Junior radials, one 11-AT conversion of a 4-AT with three 168-kW (225-hp) Packard diesel engines. Army and Navy versions were the C-3, C-4 and C-9, and the JR and RR respectively.

The legendary Ford 5-AT 'Tin Goose'

FORD 4-AT-E TRI-MOTOR
Role: Passenger transport
Crew/Accommodation: Two, plus up to 11 passengers
Power Plant: Three 300 hp Wright J-6 air-cooled radials
Dimensions: Span 22.56 m (74 ft); length 15.19 m (49.83 ft); wing area 72.93 m² (785 sq ft)
Weights: Empty 2,948 kg (6,500 lb); MTOW 4,595 kg (10,130 lb)
Performance: Cruise speed 172 km/h (107 mph) at sea level; operational ceiling 5,029 m (16,500 ft); range 917 km (570 miles)
Load: Up to 782 kg (1,725 lb)

Ford 5-AT Tri-Motor

JUNKERS Ju 52/3 (Germany)

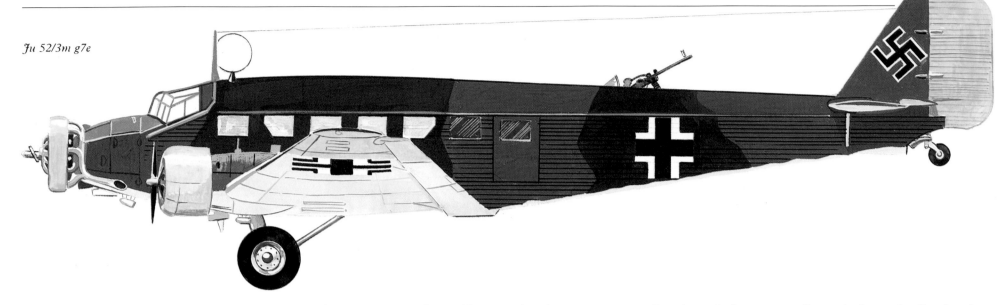

Ju 52/3m g7e

First flown in October 1930 with a single 541-kW (725-hp) BMW VII engine, the Ju 52 was produced to the extent of just six aircraft as civil transports with various engines. The type was of typical Junkers concept for the period, with corrugated alloy skinning on an angular airframe, fixed but faired tailwheel landing gear, and a low-set wing trailed by typical

Junkers full-span slotted ailerons/flaps. The Ju 52 would clearly benefit from greater power, and the company therefore developed the Ju 52/3m ce tri-motor version that first flew in April 1931 with 410-kW (550-hp) Pratt & Whitney Hornet radials. The type was produced in Ju 52/3m ce, de, fe and ge civil variants, the last with accommodation for 17 passengers on the power of three 492-kW (660-hp) BMW 132A-1 radials. Development then veered to German military needs, resulting in the Ju 52/3m g3e interim

bomber-transport pending the arrival of purpose-designed aircraft. Then the type was built as Germany's main transport and airborne forces aircraft of World War II.

The main variants in an overall production total of about 4,850 aircraft were the Ju 52/3m g4e bomber-transport with a heavier payload and a tailwheel in place of the original skid, the Ju 52/3m g5e with 619-kW (830-hp) BMW 132T-2 radials, the Ju 52/3m g6e improved transport, the Ju 52/3m g7e with an

autopilot and a larger loading hatch, Ju 52/3m g8e multi-role transport with conversion kits for specialized roles, Ju 52/3m g9e airborne forces version with a glider-tow attachment and BMW 132Z radials, Ju 52/3m g12e civil and military transport with 596-kW (800-hp) BMW 132L radials, and Ju 52/3m g14e final transport version with improved armament and armour protection. There were also small numbers of the later Ju 252 and Ju 352 developments with more power and retractable landing gear.

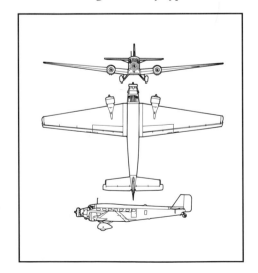

Junkers Ju 52/3m

JUNKERS Ju 52/3m g4e

Role: Military transport (land or water-based)

Crew/Accommodation: Three, plus up to 18 troops

Power Plant: Three 830 hp BMW 132T-2 air-cooled radials

Dimensions: Span 29.25 m (95.97 ft); length 18.9 m (62 ft); wing area 110.5 m² (1,189.4 sq ft)

Weights: Empty 6,510 kg (14,354 lb); MTOW 10,500 kg (23,157 lb)

Performance: Cruise speed 200 km/h (124 mph) at sea level; operational ceiling 5,000 m (18,046 ft); range 915 km (568 miles) with full payload

Load: Three 7.9 mm machine guns and up to 2,000 kg (4,409 lb) payload

Junkers Ju 52/3m floatplane in Swedish use

BOEING MODEL 247 (U.S.A.)

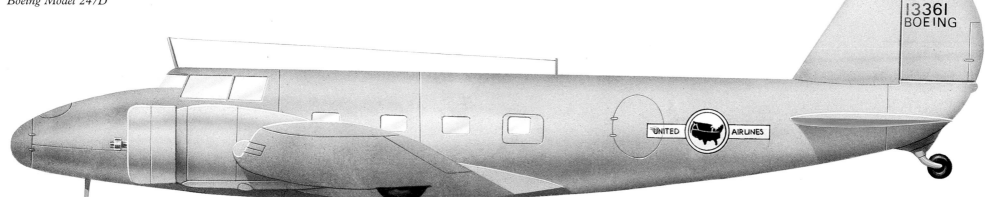

Boeing Model 247D

The Model 247 was the logical development of the other pioneering Boeing aircraft, most notably the Model 200 Monomail and Model 215. The Model 200 was a mailplane with limited passenger capacity, and introduced the cantilever monoplane wing, semi-monocoque fuselage, and retractable landing gear. The Model 215 was an extrapolation of the Model 200's concept into the bomber category, and introduced larger size and a twin-engined powerplant. The Model 247 was slightly smaller and lighter than the Model 215, and has many claims to the title of world's first 'modern' air transport as it had features such as all-metal construction, cantilever wings, pneumatic de-icing of the flying surfaces, a semi-monocoque fuselage, retractable landing gear, and fully enclosed accommodation for two pilots, a stewardess, and a planned 14 passengers. Passenger capacity was in fact limited to 10, but with this load the Model 247 could in fact both climb and maintain cruising altitude on just one engine.

The type first flew in February 1933 but, despite its undoubted technical merits, was not a great commercial success. The reasons for this were two-fold: firstly it was not available soon enough for all the airlines wishing to purchase such a modern design; and secondly the aircraft was sized to the requirement of Boeing Air Transport and therefore lacked the larger capacity needed by some potential purchasers. Thus the 60 United Air Lines examples (formed from BAT in 1931) were completed by only 15 more aircraft for companies or individuals. A Model 247ordered by Roscoe Turner and Clyde Pangbourne for the 1934 England to Australia 'MacRobertson' air race introduced drag-reducing NACA engine cowlings and controllable-pitch propellers, and these features proved so successful that they were retrofitted to most aircraft, which became the Model 247Ds.

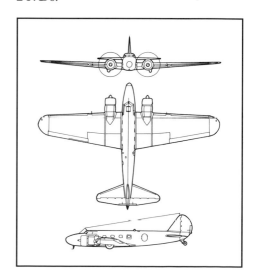

Model 247 of United Air Lines

BOEING 247D
Role: Passenger transport
Crew/Accommodation: Two crew, one cabin crew, plus up to ten passengers
Power Plant: Two 550 hp Pratt & Whitney Wasp S1H1G air-cooled radials
Dimensions: Span 22.56 m (74 ft); length 15.72 m (51.58 ft); wing area 77.67 m² (836 sq ft)
Weights: Empty 4,148 kg (9,144 lb); MTOW 6,192 kg (13,650 lb)
Performance: Cruise speed 304 km/h (189 mph); operational ceiling 7,742 m (25,400 ft); range 1,199 km (745 miles)
Load: Up to 998 kg (2,200 lb)

Boeing Model 247D

LOCKHEED L10 ELECTRA (U.S.A.)

XR20-1

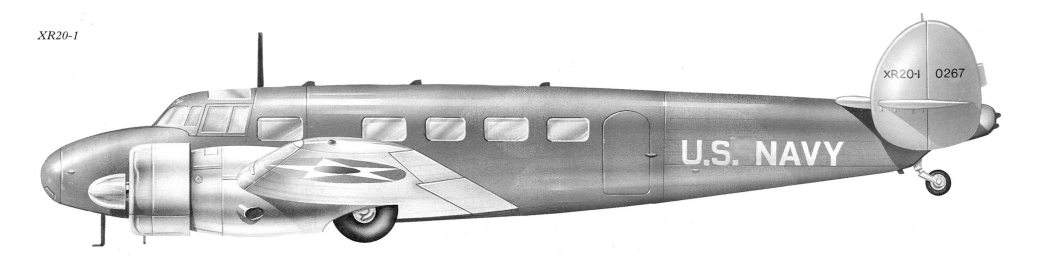

After cutting its teeth on a series of single-engined light transports that also achieved many record long-distance flights, Lockheed decided to move a step up into the potentially more lucrative twin-engined transport market with the Model 10 Electra that offered lower capacity but higher performance than contemporary Boeing and Douglas aircraft. The Electra was an advanced type of all-metal construction with endplate vertical tail surfaces, retractable tailwheel landing gear and other advanced features. The first machine flew in February 1934 with a pair of Pratt & Whitney Wasp Junior SB radials and, though the type's 10-passenger capacity was thought by many to be too small for airline operators, production totalled 148 aircraft in major variants such as 101 Electra 10-As with 336-kW (450-hp) Wasp Juniors and accommodation for 10 passengers, 18 Electra 10-Bs with 328-kW (440-hp) Wright R-975-E3 Whirlwinds, eight Electra 10-Cs with Wasp SC1s, and 15 Electra 10-Es with 447-kW (600-hp) Wasp S3H1s.

Nothing came of the projected Electra 10-D military transport, but 26 civil Electras were later impressed with the designation C-36A to C to supplement the single XC-36 high-altitude research type, three C-36s with 10-seat accommodation and the single C-37 used by the Militia Bureau. The XR2O and XR3O were single U.S. Navy and U.S. Coast Guard aircraft. The L-12 Electra Junior was a scaled-down version intended mainly for feederlines and business operators, and first flew in June 1936. Some 114 were built in Model 12 and improved Model 12-A forms with accommodation for five passengers, and many of the 73 civil aircraft were later impressed for military service. Here they shared the C-40 designation with the machines built for the U.S. Army Air Corps.

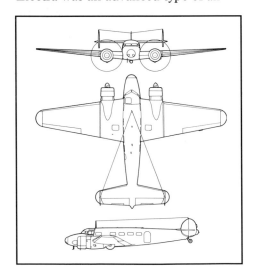

Lockheed L-10A Electra

LOCKHEED L10-A ELECTRA
Role: Passenger transport
Crew/Accommodation: Two, plus up to ten passengers
Power Plant: Two 450 hp Pratt & Whitney R-1340 Wasp Junior SB air-cooled radials
Dimensions: Span 16.76 m (55 ft); length 11.76 m (38.58 ft); wing area 42.59 m² (458.5 sq ft)
Weights: Empty 2,927 kg (6.454 lb); MTOW 4,672 kg (10,300 lb)
Performance: Maximum speed 306 km/h (190 mph) at 1,525 m (5,000 ft); operational ceiling 5,915 m (19,400 ft); range 1,305 km (810 miles)
Load: Up to 816 kg (1,800 lb)

Lockheed L-10A Electra

SIKORSKY S-42 (U.S.A.)

S-42A

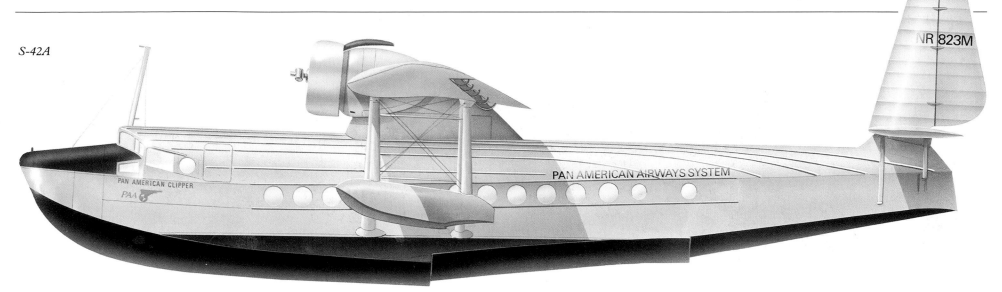

In August 1931, Pan American Airways issued a requirement for a new type of flying boat. This was needed for the transatlantic service that the airline intended to inaugurate, and called for a type carrying a crew of four and at least 12 passengers over a range of 4023 km (2,500 miles) at a cruising speed of 233 km/h (145 mph). At the end of 1932, the airline contracted with Martin for its M-130 and with Sikorsky for its S-

42. The latter was related to the S-40 amphibian to be used on Pan American's routes across the Caribbean and South America.

The S-40 had been based on the S-38 and retained the earlier design's combination of a central pod for 40 passengers and a crew of six, with a twin-boom tail and a parasol wing braced to a 'lower wing' that also supported the stabilizing floats. The

larger and more powerful S-42 was a parasol-winged flying boat with a wholly conventional boat hull, a high-set braced tailplane with twin vertical surfaces, the wing braced directly to the hull and supporting the two stabilizing floats as well as four radial engines on the leading edges. The first S-42 was delivered in August 1934, and the type flew its first service during that month between Miami and Rio de Janeiro. The type was used mainly on the airline's South American and transpacific routes (including pioneering flights across the South Pacific to New Zealand). Total

production was 10 'boats including three S-42s with the 522-kW (700-hp) Pratt & Whitney Hornet S5D1G, three-S-42A 'boats with 559-kW (750-hp) Hornet S1EG radials and longer-span wings, and four S-42B 'boats with further refinements and Hamilton Standard constant-speed propellers permitting 907-kg (2,000-lb) increase in maximum take-off weight.

The Sikorsky S-42 was based on a substantial hull

SIKORSKY S-42B
Role: Intermediate/short-range passenger transport flying boat
Crew/Accommodation: Four and two cabin crew, plus up to 32 passengers
Power Plant: Four 800 hp Pratt & Whitney R-1690 Hornet air-cooled radials
Dimensions: Span 35.97 m (118.33 ft); length 20.93 m (68.66 ft); wing area 124.5 m² (1,340 sq ft)
Weights: Empty 9,491 kg (20,924 lb); MTOW 19,504 kg (43,000 lb)
Performance: Cruise speed 225 km/h (140 mph) at 610 m (2,000 ft); operational ceiling 4,878 m (16,000 ft); range 1,207 km (750 miles) with full payload
Load: Up to 3,626 kg (7,995 lb)

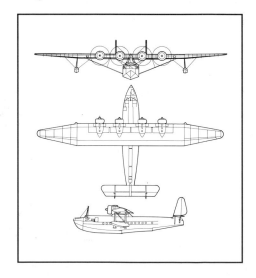

Sikorsky S-42

DOUGLAS DC3 and Military Derivatives (U.S.A.)

DC-3

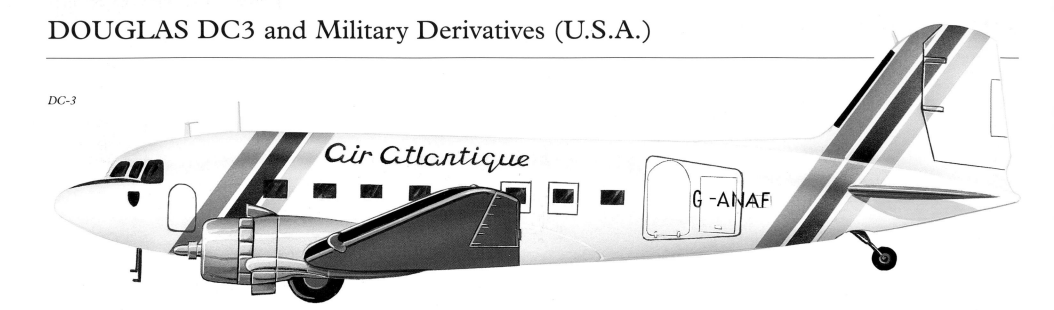

The DC-3 can truly be said to have changed history, for this type opened the era of 'modern' air travel in the mid-1930s, and became the mainstay of the Allies' air transport effort in World War II. Production of 10,349 aircraft was completed in the United States; at least another 2,000 were produced under licence in the U.S.S.R. as the Lisunov Li-2, and 485 were built in Japan as the Showa

(Nakajima) L2D.

The series began with the DC-1 that first flew in July 1933 as a cantilever low-wing monoplane of all-metal construction (except fabric-covered control surfaces) with enclosed accommodation and features such as retractable landing gear and trailing-edge flaps. From this prototype was developed the 14-passenger DC-2 production model, which was built in modest numbers but paved the way for the Douglas Sleeper Transport that first flew in December 1935 as an airliner for

transcontinental night flights with 16 passengers in sleeper berths. From this was evolved the 24-passenger DC-3. This latter was produced in five series with either the Wright SGR-1820 Cyclone or Pratt & Whitney R-1830 Twin Wasp radial as the standard engine. The type was ordered for the U.S. military as the C-47 Skytrain (U.S. Army) and R4D (U.S. Navy), while the British adopted the name Dakota for aircraft supplied under the terms of the Lend-Lease Act.

The type was produced in a vast number of variants within the new-build C-47, C-53, C-117 and R4D series for transport, paratrooping, and glider-towing duties, while impressed aircraft swelled numbers and also designations to a bewildering degree. After the war, large quantities of these monumentally reliable aircraft were released cheaply to civil operators, and the series can be credited with the development of air transport in most of the world's remoter regions.

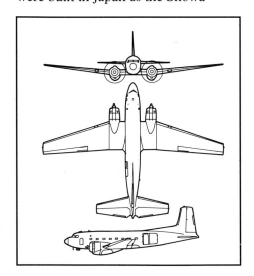

Douglas R4D-8

DOUGLAS DC-3A
Role: Passenger transport
Crew/Accommodation: Three, plus two cabin crew and up to 28 passengers
Power Plant: Two 1,200 hp Pratt & Whitney Twin Wasp S1C3-G air cooled radials
Dimensions: Span 28.96 m (95 ft); length 19.65 m (64.47 ft); wing area 91.7 m² (987 sq ft)
Weights: Empty 7,650 g (16,865 lb); MTOW 11,431 kg (25,200 lb)
Performance: Maximum speed 370 km/h (230 mph) at 2,590 m (8,500 sq ft); operational ceiling 7,070 m (23,200 ft); range 3,420 km (2,125 miles)
Load: Up to 2,350 kg (5,180 lb)

A Douglas DC-3 in service with East African Airways

FOCKE-WULF Fw 200 CONDOR (Germany)

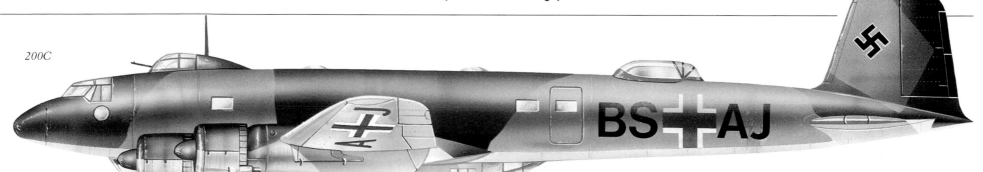

200C

The Fw 200 was developed as a transatlantic passenger and mail aircraft that might appeal to Deutsche Lufthansa. The first of three prototypes flew during July 1937 with 652-kW (750-hp) Pratt and Whitney Hornet radials and room for a maximum of 26 passengers in two cabins; the next two aircraft had 537-kW (720-hp) BMW 132G-1 radials. Eight Fw 200A pre-production transports were delivered to Lufthansa and single examples to Brazilian and Danish airliners. Four Fw 200B airliners with 619-kW (830-hp) BMW 132H engines followed. Some of these later became the personal transports of Nazi VIPs.

The Condor's real claim to fame rests with its Fw 200C series, Germany's most important maritime reconnaissance bomber of World War II. This was pioneered by a maritime reconnaissance prototype ordered by Japan but never delivered. Ten Fw 200C-0 pre-production aircraft were delivered as six maritime reconnaissance and four transport aircraft, and there followed a steadily more diverse sequence of specialized aircraft that were hampered by a structural weakness in the fuselage aft of the wing but nevertheless played a major part in the Atlantic and Arctic convoy campaigns. The Fw 200C-1 was a reconnaissance bomber with a 1750-kg (3,757-lb) bomb load, and the Fw 200C-2 was an aerodynamically refined variant. The Fw 200C-3 had 895-kW (1,200-hp) BMW-Bramo 323R-2 Fafnir radials, structural strengthening, and improved defensive and offensive armament in four subvariants. The main model was the Fw 200C-4 with radar, and there were two 11- and 14-passenger transport derivatives of this. The Fw 200C-6 was the C-3 modified as launcher for two Henschel Hs 293 anti-ship missiles, while the Fw 200C-8 was another missile carrier with improved radar. Total production was 276 aircraft.

The Fw 200 V5

FOCKE-WULF Fw 200C-3 CONDOR
Role: Long-range maritime reconnaisance bomber
Crew: Accommodation: Seven
Power Plant: Four 1,200-hp BMW Bramo 323 R-2 Fafnir air-cooled radials
Dimensions: Span 32.84 m (107.74 ft); length 23.85 m (78.25 ft); wing area 118m² (1,290 sq ft)
Weights: Empty 17,000 kg (37,485 lb); MTOW 22,700 kg (50,045 lb)
Performance: Cruise speed 335 km/h (208 mph) at 4,000 m (13,124 ft); operational ceiling 6,000 m (19,685 ft); range 3,560 km (2,211 miles)
Load: One 20-mm cannon, three 13-mm and two 7.9-mm machine guns, plus up to 2,100 kg (4,630 lb) of bombs

Focke-Wulf Fw 200C-1 Condor

DORNIER Do 26 (Germany)

Dornier Do 26

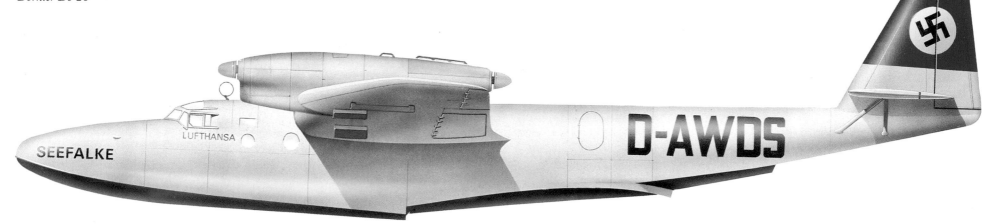

Dornier built many types of flying boat, but the type that offered the cleanest aerodynamics and the most pleasing lines was, without doubt, the Do 26. The type had its origins in the transatlantic mail services developed in the 1930s, and was designed to carry a flight crew of four and 500 kg (1,102 lb) of mail between Lisbon and New York. The all-metal design was based on a slender two-step hull carrying a shoulder-mounted gull wing

and a simple tail unit with braced tailplane halves. The four engines were located in the angles of the gull wings as push/pull tandem pairs in single nacelles that offered minimum resistance. Junkers Jumo 205C/D diesel engines each delivering 447-kW (600-hp) were chosen for their reliability and low specific fuel consumption, and the two pusher engines were installed on mountings that allowed them to be tilted up at

10° at take-off so that the three-blade propeller units were clear of the spray from the hull.

The flying boats were stressed for catapult launches from support ships, and Deutsche Lufthansa ordered three aircraft during 1937. The first of these flew in May 1938, and the two machines completed before the outbreak of World War II were delivered to the airline with the designation Do 26A. These were never used for their intended North Atlantic route, and completed just 18 crossings of the South Atlantic. The third machine was to have been the

Do 26B with provision for four passengers, but was completed as the first of an eventual four Do 26D military flying boats in the long-range reconnaissance and transport roles. These were powered by 522-kW (700-hp) Jumo 205Ea engines, and carried a bow turret armed with a single 20-mm cannon in addition to three 7.92-mm (0.312-in) machine guns in one dorsal and two waist positions.

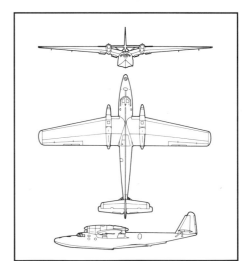

In the air, the Dornier Do 26 had very clean lines

DORNIER Do 26A
Role: Long-range mail transport
Crew/Accommodation: Four
Power Plant: Four 700 hp Junkers Jumo 205C liquid-cooled diesels
Dimensions: Span 30.00 m (98.42 ft); length 24.60 m (80.71 ft); wing area 120 m² (1,291.67 sq ft)
Weights: Empty 10,700 kg (23,594 lb); MTOW 20,000 kg (44,100 lb)
Performance: Maximum speed 335 km/h (208 mph) at sea level; operational ceiling 4,800 m (15,748 ft); range 9,000 km (5,592 miles) with full payload
Load: Up to 500 kg (1,103 lb)

Dornier Do 26 V4

BOEING 314 (U.S.A.)

Boeing Model 314A

The Model 314 was the greatest flying boat ever built for the civil air transport role. It was designed to the requirement of Pan American Airways for the transatlantic service which the airline had requested from the U.S. Bureau of Air Commerce as early as January 1935. The airline already operated the Martin M-130 and Sikorsky S-42 flying boat airliners, but wanted a 'state-of-the-art' type for this new prestige route. Boeing designed its Model 314 on the basis of the wings and modified tailplane of the Model 294 (XB-15) experimental bomber married to a fuselage accommodating a maximum of 74 passengers in four cabins. The engines were a quartet of 1119-kW (1,500-hp) Wright GR-2600 Double Cyclone radials with fuel for a range of 5633 km (3,500 miles). Some of the fuel was stored in the two lateral sponsons that stabilized the machine on the water and also served as loading platforms.

The first aeroplane flew in June 1938, and the original single vertical tail was soon replaced by twin endplate surfaces that were then supplemented by a central fin based on the original vertical surface but without a movable rudder. The Model 314 entered service in May 1939 as a mailplane, and the first passengers were carried in June of the same year. The six Model 314s were later joined by six Model 314As (including three for the British Overseas Airways Corporation) with more fuel and 1193-kW (1,600-hp) engines driving larger-diameter propellers. Six of the aircraft were used in World War II by the American military in the form of C-98s and B-314s.

Boeing Model 314

BOEING 314A
Role: Long-range passenger flying boat
Crew/Accommodation: Three, plus seven cabin crew and up to 74 passengers
Power Plant: Four 1,600 hp Wright GR-2600 Double Cyclone air-cooled radials
Dimensions: Span 46.33 m (152 ft); length 32.31 m (106 ft); wing area 266.35 m² (2,867 sq ft)
Weights: Empty 22,801 kg (50,268 lb); MTOW 37,422 kg (82,500 lb)
Performance: Cruise speed 295 km/h (183 mph) at sea level; operational ceiling 4,084 m (13,400 ft); range 5,632 km (3,500 miles)
Load: Up to 6,713 kg (14,800 lb)

The Boeing Model 314 was undoubtedly the finest flying boat airliner ever built

LOCKHEED CONSTELLATION Family (U.S.A.)

EC-121K

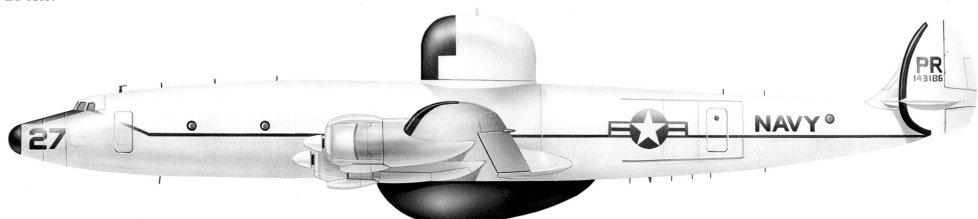

This was surely one of the classic aircraft of all time, developed as an elegant yet efficient airliner but also of great military importance as the basis of the world's first long-range airborne early warning and electronic warfare aircraft. The design was originated in 1939 to provide Pan American Airways and Transcontinental and Western Air with an advanced airliner for use on long-range domestic routes.

The Lockheed design was centred on refined aerodynamics, pressurized accommodation and high power for sustained high-altitude cruising at high speed, and tricycle landing gear was incorporated for optimum field performance and passenger comfort on the ground.

The type first flew in January 1943, and civil production was overtaken by the needs of the military during World War II; the L-49 thus became the U.S. Army's C-69, of which 22 were completed before Japan's capitulation

and the cancellation of military orders. Some aircraft then on the production line were completed as 60-seat L-049 airliners, but the first true civil version was the 81-seat L-649 with 1864-kW (2,500-hp) Wright 749C-18BD-1 radials. Further airliners were the L-749 with additional fuel, the L-1049 Super Constellation with the fuselage lengthened by 5.59 m (18 in 4 in) for the accommodation of 109 passengers, and the L-1649 Starliner with a new, longer-span wing and 2535-kW (3,500-hp) Wright 988TC-

18EA-2 radials fed from increased fuel tankage for true intercontinental range. Production of the series totalled 856 including military variants that included the C-121 transport version of the L-749, the R7O naval transport version of the L-1049, and the PO-1 and VW-2 Warning Star airborne early warning aircraft. These R7O, PO-1 and VW-2 aircraft were later redesignated in the C-121 series that expanded to include a large number of EC-121 electronic warfare aircraft.

Lockheed L-749 Constellation

LOCKHEED L749 CONSTELLATION
Role: Long-range passenger transport
Crew/Accommodation: Four and two cabin crew, plus up to 81 passengers
Power Plant: Four 2,500 hp Wright 749C-18BD-1 Double Cyclone air-cooled radials
Dimensions: Span 37.49 m (123 ft); length 29.03 m (95.25 ft); wing area 153.3 m² (1,650 sq ft)
Weights: Empty 27,648 kg (60,954 lb); MTOW 47,627 (105,000 lb)
Performance: Cruise speed 557 km/h (346 mph) at 9,072 m (20,000 ft); operational ceiling 10,886 m (24,000 ft); range 3,219 km/h (2,000 miles) with 6,124 (13,500 lb) payload plus reserves
Load: Up to 6,690 kg (14,750 lb) with 6,124 kg (13,500 lb)

This is an L-049E named Baltimore

CONVAIR CONVAIRLINER Series (U.S.A.)

Convair 440

The CV-240 series was developed in the hope of producing a successor to the legendary Douglas DC-3, and though the type was in every respect good, with features such as pressurized accommodation and tricycle landing gear that kept the fuselage level on the ground, it failed to make a decisive impression on a market saturated by the vast number of C-47s released on to the civil market when they became surplus to military requirements. The spur for the type's original design was a specification issued in 1945 by American Airlines for a modern airliner to supersede the DC-3 and offer superior operating economics.

The CV-110 prototype first flew in July 1946 with 1566-kW (2,100-hp) Pratt & Whitney R-2800-S1C3-G radial engines and pressurized accommodation for 30 passengers. Even before this prototype flew, however, American Airlines had revised its specification and now demanded greater capacity. It proved a comparatively straightforward task to increase capacity to 40 passengers by lengthening the fuselage by 1.12 m (3 ft 8 in), and in this form the airliner became the CV-240. No prototype was built, the company flying its first production example in March 1947. The CV-240 entered service in June 1948, and 176 were built as airliners. There followed the 44-passenger CV-340 with 1864-kW (2,500-hp) R-2800-CB-16 or 17 engines and a fuselage stretch of 1.37 m (4 ft 6 in), and finally the similar CV-440 with aerodynamic refinements and high-density seating for 52 passengers. Turboprop conversions were later made to produce the CV-540, 580, 600 and 640 series. Variants for the military were the T-29 USAF crew trainer, the C-131 air ambulance and transport for the USAF, and the R4Y transport for the U.S. Navy.

CV-440 Metropolitan

CONVAIR 440 CONVAIRLINER
Role: Short-range passenger transport
Crew/Accommodation: Two, plus up to 52 passengers
Power Plant: Two 2,500 hp Pratt & Whitney R-2800-CB16/17 Double Wasp air-cooled radials
Dimensions: Span 31.10 m (105. 33 ft); length 24.84 m (81.5 ft); wing area 85.47 m² (920 sq ft)
Weights: Empty 15,111 kg (33,314 lb); MTOW 22,544 kg (49.700 lb)
Performance: Cruise speed 465 km/h (289 mph) at 6,096 m (20,000 ft); operational ceiling 7,590 m (24,900 ft); range 459 km (285 miles) with maximum payload
Load: Up to 5,820 kg (12,836 lb)

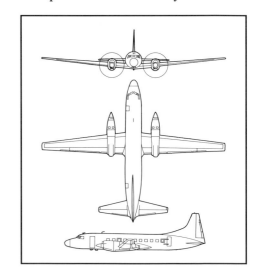

Convair CV-580

AIRSPEED AMBASSADOR (United Kingdom)

AS.57 Ambassador

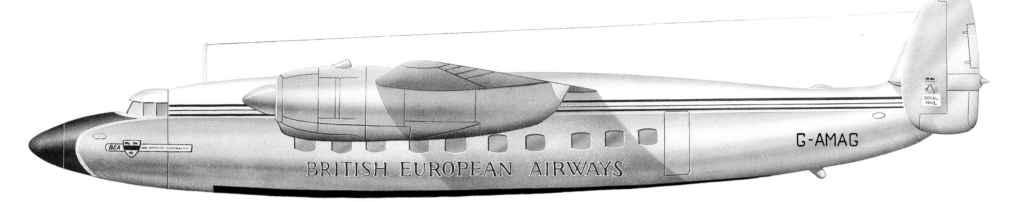

The Ambassador was one of the most elegant aircraft ever built, and resulted from the Brabazon Committee's 1943 recommendation for a 30-seat short/medium-range airliner to be built after World War II within the context of reviving the U.K.'s airline network and civil aircraft production capability. The AS.57 was designed in the closing stages of the war with a high aspect ratio wing set high on the circular-

section pressurized fuselage, which ended in an upswept tail unit with triple vertical surfaces; the main units of the tricycle landing gear retracted into the rear part of the two engine nacelles slung under the inner portions of the wing.

The first Ambassador flew in July 1947 and, with two Bristol Centaurus radials, had very promising performance. Just over one year later, an order for 20 aircraft was received from BEA, but the programme was then beset by a number of technical problems during its development. This delayed the Ambassador's service entry until March 1952, and meant

that the initial 20-aircraft order was the only one fulfilled as this piston-engined type had been overtaken in performance and operating economics by the turboprop-powered Vickers Viscount. Even so, the 'Elizabethan' class served BEA with great popularity

for six years, and the aircraft were then acquired by five other operators. The second and third prototypes went on to important subsidiary careers as test beds for turboprops, such as the Bristol Proteus, the Napier Eland, and the Rolls-Royce Dart and Tyne.

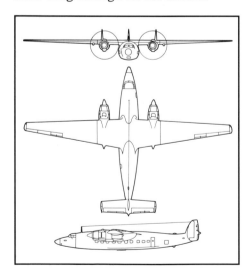

Airspeed AS.57 Ambassador

AIRSPEED AMBASSADOR
Role: Short range passenger transport
Crew/Accommodation: Three, plus three cabin crew and 47/49 passengers
Power Plant: Two 2,700 hp Bristol Centaurus 661 air-cooled radials
Dimensions: Span 35.05 m (115 ft); length 24.69 m (81 ft); wing area 111.48 m² (1,200 sq ft)
Weights: Empty 16,277 kg (35,884 lb); MTOW 23,590 kg (52,000 lb)
Performance: Cruise speed 483 km/h (300 mph) at 6,096 m (20,000 ft); range 1,159 km (720 miles) with maximum payload
Load: Up to 5,285 kg (11,650 lb)

The Airspeed Ambassador was a design of aerodynamic elegance

BOEING STRATOCRUISER and C-97 Series (U.S.A.)

Stratocruiser

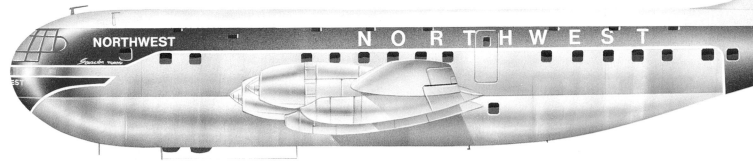

The Model 377 was a commercial transport developed from the C-97 military transport, which itself evolved as the Model 367 to combine the wings, engines, tail unit, landing gear and lower fuselage of the B-29 bomber with a new upper fuselage lobe of considerably larger radius and so create a pressurized 'double-bubble' fuselage. This provided considerable volume, and also provided the Model 377 with its distinctive two-deck layout. The Model 377-10-9 prototype was based on the YC-97A with Pratt & Whitney R-4360 radial engines, and first flew in July 1947.

The aircraft was later delivered to Pan American Airways, which soon became the world's largest operator of the Stratocruiser, with 27 of the 55 aircraft built. Ten of them were fitted with additional fuel tankage as Super Stratocruisers, and these were suitable for the transatlantic route. At a later date, all Pan Am's aircraft were modified with a General Electric CH-10 turbocharger on each engine for an additional 37.3 kW (50 hp) of power for high-altitude cruise. The other major operator of the type was BOAC, which bought six new aircraft and then found this particular type so useful that is secured another 11 from other operators.

The Stratocruiser was available in Model 377-10-26, -28, -29, -30 and -32 variants with interior arrangements that catered for anything between 58 and 112 day passengers, or alternatively 33 night passengers accommodated in five seats as well as 28 upper- and lower-deck berths. The standard accommodation was on the upper deck, with access to the 14-person cocktail lounge on the lower deck via a spiral staircase.

Strange derivatives of the C-97/Stratocruiser became the Guppy series of 'outsized' transports developed by Aero Spacelines, starting with the Pregnant Guppy in 1962. Each featured a huge fuselage extension to allow carriage of very bulky freight.

The Aero Spacelines Guppy-201

BOEING 377 STRATOCRUISER
Role: Long range passenger transport
Crew/Accommodation: Five and five cabin crew, plus up to 95 passengers
Power Plant: Four 3,500 hp Pratt & Whitney R-4360B3 Double Wasp air-cooled radials
Dimensions: 43.03 m (141.19 ft); length 33.63 m (110.33 ft); wing area 159.79 m² (1,720 sq ft)
Weights: Empty 35,797 kg (78,920 lb); MTOW 67,131 kg (148,000 lb)
Performance: Maximum speed 603 km/h (375 mph) at 7,625 m (25,000 ft); operational ceiling 9,754 m (32,000 ft); range 7,360 km (4,600 miles) with full fuel
Load: Up to 13,608 kg (30,000 lb)

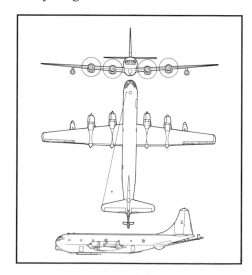

KC-97G Stratofreighter

23

de HAVILLAND CANADA DHC-2 BEAVER (Canada)

DHC-2 Beaver

The only model to achieve mass production was the Beaver I, of which 1,657 were produced with the ability to carry the pilot and a basic payload of seven passengers or 680 kg (1,500 lb) of freight. No fewer than 980 of these Beaver Is were bought by the U.S. Army and U.S. Air Force with the basic designation L-20 (from 1962 U-6); six were YL-20 service test aircraft, 968 were L-20A production aircraft, and six were L-20B production aircraft with different equipment. One Beaver II was produced with the 410-kW (550-hp) Alvis Leonides radial, and there were also a few Turbo-Beaver IIIs with the 431-kW (578-ehp) Pratt & Whitney Canada PT6A-6/20 turboprop and provision for 10 passengers. Production of this classic type ended in the mid-1960s as de Havilland Canada concentrated on more ambitious aircraft.

The DHC-2 Beaver was designed from 1946 specifically to meet a specification issued by the Ontario Department of Lands and Forests, and resulted in a superb aircraft that fully met the overall Canadian need for a bushplane to replace pre-World War II types such as the Noorduyn Norseman and various Fairchild aircraft. Key features of the design were the rugged reliability of the airframe and single radial engine, STOL performance, operational versatility, and the ability to carry wheels, skis, or floats on the main units of its tailwheel landing gear, whose wide track gave the type exceptional stability on the ground, snow, or water. The DHC-2 was designed round the readily available and thoroughly reliable Pratt & Whitney R-985 Wasp Junior engine, and emerged for its first flight in August 1947 as a braced high-wing monoplane together with sturdy fixed landing gear.

de Havilland Canada DHC-2 Beaver

de HAVILLAND CANADA DHC-2 BEAVER I
Role: Light utility transport
Crew/Accommodation: One, plus up to six passengers
Power Plant: One 450 hp Pratt & Whitney R-985AN-6B Wasp Junior air-cooled radial
Dimensions: 14.62 m (48.00 ft); length 9.23 m (30.25 ft); wing area 23.20 m² (250.00 sq ft)
Weights: Empty 1,294 kg (2,850 lb); MTOW 2,313 kg (5,100 lb)
Performance: Maximum speed 257 km/h (160 mph) at 1,524 m (5,000 ft); operational ceiling 5,486 m (18,000 ft); range 756 km (470 miles) with full payload
Load: Up to 613 kg (1,350 lb)

The de Havilland Canada DHC-2 Beaver

DOUGLAS DC-7 (U.S.A.)

Douglas DC-7C

In its C-54 military guise, the DC-4 proved an invaluable long-range transport in World War II. The type's reliability is attested by the fact that only three aircraft were lost in the course of 80,000 or more oceanic crossings. Capacity was limited, however, and Douglas developed to army order the similar but pressurized XC-112A with a longer fuselage. This first flew in February 1946 and was thus too late for the war. With no military orders forthcoming, Douglas

marketed the type as the civil DC-6 that later spawned a military C-118 Liftmaster derivative. And from the DC-6B passenger transport, the company developed the DC-7 to meet an American Airlines' requirement for an airliner to compete with TWA's Lockheed Super Constellation. The DC-7 had a lengthened fuselage, beefed-up landing gear and the same 2424-kW (3,250-hp) Wright R-3350 Turbo-Compound engines as the Super Constellation.

The type first flew in May 1953 and entered production as the DC-6 transcontinental transport, of which 105 were built. To provide transatlantic range, Douglas developed the DC-7B with additional fuel capacity in longer engine nacelles. Production of this variant totalled 112 aircraft, but the model proved to possess only marginally adequate capability in its intended role, and was therefore superseded by the DC-7C, often called the Seven Seas. This became one of the definitive piston-engined airliners, and production

totalled 120. The type had 2535-kW (3,400-hp) R-3350-18EA-1 engines, a fuselage lengthened by 1.02 m (3 ft 4 in) to allow the carriage of 105 passengers and, most importantly, increased fuel capacity in parallel-chord inboard wing extensions that also possessed the additional benefit of moving the engines farther from the fuselage and so reducing cabin noise.

This was the thirtieth Douglas DC-7 to be built

DOUGLAS DC-7C
Role: Long-range passenger transport
Crew/Accommodation: Four and four/five cabin crew, plus up to 105 passengers
Power Plant: Four 3,400 hp Wright R-3350-18EA-1 Turbo-Compound air-cooled radials
Dimensions: Span 38.86 m (127.5 ft); length 34.21 m (112.25 ft); wing area 152.08 m² (1,637 sq ft)
Weights: Empty 33,005 kg (72,763 lb); MTOW 64,864 kg (143,000 lb)
Performance: Cruise speed 571 km/h (355 mph) at 5,791 m (19,000 ft); operational ceiling 6,615 m (21,700 ft); range 7,410 km (4,605 miles) with maximum payload
Load: Up to 10,591 kg (23,350 lb)

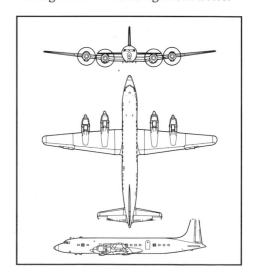

Douglas DC-7C

BRITTEN-NORMAN BN2 ISLANDER Family (United Kingdom)

BN2A Islander

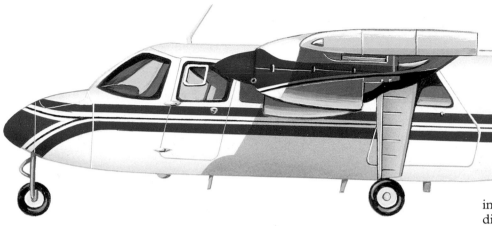

The Islander was designed as a simple feederliner for operators in remoter areas, and was schemed as a low-maintenance type of all-metal construction with fixed tricycle landing gear, a high-set wing mounting the two reliable piston engines, and a slab-sided fuselage with 'wall-to-wall' seating accessed by one door on the starboard side and two on the port side. The first Islander flew in June 1965 with two 157-kW (210-hp) Continental IO-360-B engines. The type was underpowered and had too high a wing loading. This meant the adoption of a wing spanning 1.22 m (4 ft 0 in) more, and a power plant of two 194-kW (260-hp) Lycoming O-540-E engines. The result was the BN2 model that entered service in August 1967.

Later variants became the refined BN2A and the heavier BN2B with an interior of proved design and smaller-diameter propellers for lower cabin noise levels. Options have included an extended nose providing additional baggage volume. The current piston-engined models are the BN2B-26 and the BN2B-20, the latter with more powerful engines. The type has also been produced in Defender and other militarized models with underwing hardpoints, and options for weapons and/or sensors that can optimize the aircraft for a number of important roles in the electronic warfare arena. Turbine power became an increasingly attractive alternative during the Islander's early production career, and the result was the BN2T with two 239-kW (320-shp) Allison 250-B17C turboprops, which remains available. The largest derivative became the Trislander with a third engine added at the junction of the enlarged vertical tail and the mid-set tailplane. The Trislander was given a lengthened fuselage for 17 passengers.

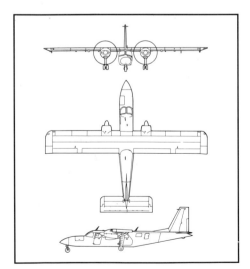

BN2A Islander

BRITTEN-NORMAN BN2B-20
Role: Light short-field utility/passenger transport
Crew/Accommodation: One, plus up to nine passengers
Power Plant: Two 260 hp Lycoming O-540-E4C5 air-cooled flat-opposed
Dimensions: Span 14.94 m (49 ft); length 10.97 m (36 ft); wing area 30.2 m² (325 sq ft)
Weights: Empty 1,866 kg (4,114 lb); MTOW 2,993 kg (6,600 lb)
Performance: Cruise speed 263 km/h (164 mph) at 2,440 m (8,000 ft); operational ceiling 3,444 m (11,300 ft); range 1,763 km (1,096 miles) with optional wingtip tanks for IFR flying
Load: Up to 1,082 kg (2.386 lb) disposable load

The triple-engined Britten-Norman Trislander

Britten-Norman BN2B Islander, operated by British Airways Express

Civil Turboprop-Engined Transports

It was as long ago as 1926 that British Dr A.A. Griffith first suggested that a turbine engine could be used to produce not only jet exhaust but the power needed to turn a propeller via a reduction gear. During World War II Rolls-Royce developed its Derwent turbojet engine and, from this, conceived a turboprop derivative as the Trent, which drove a five-blade propeller. Incredibly, an early Gloster Meteor fighter prototype was used to flight-test the Trent, in September 1945, and thereby became the first aeroplane in history to fly on turboprop power alone.

The wartime Brabazon Committee recommended that a turboprop-powered short/medium-range airliner should be developed among other types, and what was originally named the Brabazon IIB eventually appeared in 1948 as the Vickers Viscount, the world's first turbine-powered airliner of either turboprop or turbojet varieties. The Dart engines chosen provided the required mix of high performance and fuel economy and, although virtually all large commercial jetliners were eventually to adopt turbojets for greatest performance gains from turbine power, turboprops remained the favoured engine type for many of the smaller airliners to this day. Of course, it should not be overlooked that some of the world's largest aircraft have also used turboprop power, including giant Soviet and Ukrainian types, while another historic first for

turboprop power came in December 1957 when a BOAC Bristol Britannia 312 flew from London to New York and was thereby the first-ever turbine airliner to undertake a transatlantic passenger service.

Bringing older aircraft up to required modern standards of performance has included DC-3s being re-engined with turboprops. Here a Balser Turbo-67 (DC-3 type) has a lengthened fuselage, twin Pratt & Whitney Canada PT6A turboprops and other updates, thereby offering 76 per cent more productivity than a standard piston-engined DC-3 plus many other benefits.

VICKERS VISCOUNT (United Kingdom)

Viscount 800

The Type 630 Viscount was the world's first turbine-powered airliner to enter service. The aircraft was developed as the Vickers VC2 (originally the Brabazon IIB) to meet a requirement for a 24-seat short/medium-range airliner with a turboprop powerplant. The specification was issued during World War II by the Brabazon Committee that was charged with assessing the U.K.'s post-war civil air transport needs, and the prototype

Type 630 was designed as a 32-passenger airliner of attractive design and orthodox construction based on a cantilever low-wing monoplane layout with retractable tricycle landing gear.

The first example flew in July 1948 with four 738-kW (990-shp) Rolls-Royce Dart RDa.1 Mk 502 turboprops in slim wing-mounted nacelles. The type had too low a capacity to attract any real commercial interest, but was then revised in

accordance with the requirement of British European Airways for an airliner with pressurized accommodation for between 40 and 59 passengers. This Type 700 became the first production version with a powerplant of four 1044-kW (1,400-shp) Dart Mk 506s or, in the Type 700D, four 1193-kW (1,600-shp) Dart Mk 510s. These latter engines also powered the Type 800 with a lengthened fuselage for between 65 and 71 passengers. The Type 810 was structurally strengthened for operation at higher weights, and was powered by 1566-kW (2,100-shp) Dart RDa.7/1

Mk 525s. Total production was eventually 444 aircraft, and the type made the world's first turbine-powered commercial airline flight on 29 July 1950 at the beginning of a two-week experimental service between London and Paris. The Viscount was sold in many parts of the world, and made good though not decisive inroads into the lucrative American market.

A Vickers Viscount 785 of Alitalia

VICKERS VISCOUNT 810
Role: Short-range passenger transport
Crew/Accommodation: Three and two cabin crew, plus up to 71 passengers
Power Plant: Four 2,100 shp Rolls-Royce Dart R.Da 7/1 Mk. 525 turboprops
Dimensions: Span 28.5 m (93.76 ft); length 26.11 m (85.66 ft); wing area 89.46 m² (963 sq ft)
Weights: Empty 18,753 kg (41,565 lb); MTOW 32,886 kg (72,500 lb)
Performance: Maximum speed 563 km/h (350 mph) at 6,100 m (20,000 ft); operational ceiling 7,620 m (25,000 ft); range 2,775 km (1,725 miles) with maximum payload
Load: Up to 6,577 kg (14,500 lb)

Vickers Viscount 800

BRISTOL BRITANNIA (United Kingdom)

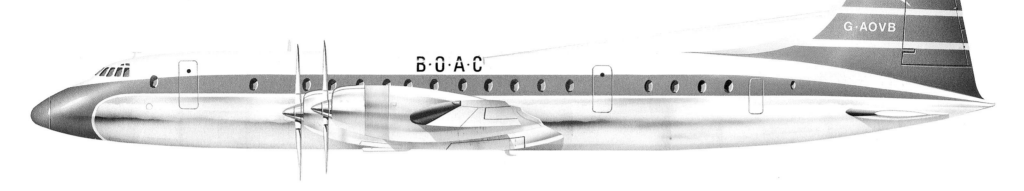

Britannia

Probably the finest turboprop airliner ever built, the Britannia was so delayed by engine problems that it was overtaken by jet-powered airliners and thus failed to fulfil its great commercial promise. The type was one of eight types proposed by five companies to meet a BOAC requirement shortly after the end of World War II for a Medium-Range Empire airliner with pressurized accommodation for 36 passengers. The Type 175's proposed powerplant of four Bristol Centaurus radials was more than adequate for the specified load, so the design was enlarged to 48-passenger capacity. The Ministry of Supply ordered three prototypes, but the design was further amended and, when the first machine flew in August 1952, it had provision for 90 passengers on the power of four 2088-kW (2,800-ehp) Bristol Proteus turboprops. This paved the way for the first production model, the Britannia Series 100 which entered service in 1957 with 2819-kW (3,780-ehp) Proteus 705s; 15 of these were built for BOAC.

There followed eight Britannia Series 300s with the fuselage lengthened by 3.12 m (10 ft 3 in) for a maximum of 133 passengers carried over transatlantic routes, and 32 Britannia Series 310s with 3072-kW (4,120-ehp) Proteus 755s and greater fuel capacity. Only two were built of the final Britannia Series 320 with 3318-kW (4,450-ehp) Proteus 765s, while production of the Britannia for the civil market in total numbered just 60 aircraft. The last variant was the Britannia Series 250 modelled on the Series 310 but intended for RAF use as 20 Britannia C.Mk 1s and three C.Mk 2s. Exactly the same basic airframe was used by Canadair as the core of two aircraft, the CL-28 Argus maritime patroller with 2535-kW (3,400-hp) Wright R-3350-EA1 Turbo-Compound piston engines, together with the CL-44 long-range transport with 4273-kW (5,730-ehp) Rolls-Royce Tyne 515 Mk 10 turboprops.

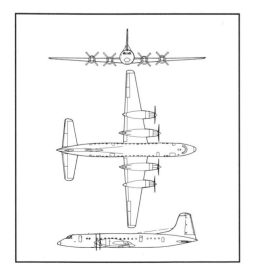

Bristol Britannia 320

BRISTOL BRITANNIA 310 Series
Role: Long-range passenger transport
Crew/Accommodation: Four, four cabin crew and up to 139 passengers
Power Plant: Four 4,120 ehp Bristol Siddeley Proteus 755 turboprops
Dimensions: Span 43.37 m (142.29 ft); length 37.87 m (124.25 ft); wing area 192.78 m² (2,075 sq ft)
Weights: Empty 37,438 kg (82,537 lb); MTOW 83,915 kg (185,000 lb)
Performance: Cruise speed 660 km/h (410 mph) at 6,401 m (21,000 ft); operational ceiling 9,200+ m (30,184 ft); range 6,869 km (4,268 miles) with maximum payload
Load: Up to 15,830 kg (34,900 lb)

A Bristol Britannia 253F

FOKKER F.27 FRIENDSHIP and 50 (Netherlands)

F.27 Mk 200 Friendship

After World War II Fokker sought to recapture a slice of the airliner market with a type matching the best of its classic interwar airliners. After long deliberation, the company fixed on a short/medium-range type powered by two Rolls-Royce Dart turboprops on the high-set wing. The first of two prototypes flew in November 1955. The Friendship entered service in December 1958 as the F.27 Mk 100 with two 1279-kW (1,715-shp) Dart RDa. 6 Mk 514-7 engines for the carriage of between 40 and 52 passengers, and was followed by successively upgraded models such as the F.27 Mk 200 with 1529-kW (2,050-shp) Dart RDa. 7 Mk 532-7 engines, the F.27 Mks 300 and 400 Combiplane derivatives of the Mks 100 and 200 with reinforced cabin floors and a large cargo door on the port side of the forward fuselage. The F.27 Mk 500 introduced a fuselage lengthened by 1.50 m (4ft 11 in) for between 52 and 60 passengers. The last variant was the F.27 Mk 600 convertible variant of the Mk 400 without the reinforced floor.

Military variants became the F.27 Mks 400M and 500M Troopship, and specialized maritime reconnaissance models were the unarmed F.27 Maritime and armed F.27 Maritime Enforcer. F.27 production ended with the 579th aircraft, which was delivered in 1987. The basic Mks 100, 200 and 300 were licence-built in the United States as the Fairchild F-27A, B and C to the extent of 128 aircraft, and the same company also produced a variant with its fuselage stretched by 1.83m (6 ft 0 in) as the FH-227, of which 79 were produced.

The durability of the Friendship's basic design was attested by the follow-up development of the Fokker 50, a thoroughly updated 58-passenger version with Pratt & Whitney Canada PW125B or PW127B turboprops driving six-blade propellers. The first Fokker 50 was delivered in August 1987.

A Fokker F.27 Mk 600R Friendship

FOKKER 50
Role: Short-range passenger transport
Crew/Accommodation: Two and two cabin crew, plus up to 58 passengers
Power Plant: Two 2,250 shp Pratt & Whitney PW 125B turboprops
Dimensions: Span 29 m (95.15 ft); length 25.25 m (82.83 ft); wing area 70 m² (754 sq ft)
Weights: Empty 12,741 kg (28.090 lb); MTOW 18,990 kg (41,865 lb)
Performance: Cruise speed 500 km/h (270 knots) at 6,096 m (20,000 ft); operational ceiling 7,620 m (25,000 ft); range 1,125 km (607 naut. miles) with 50 passengers
Load: Up to 5,262 kg (11,600 lb)

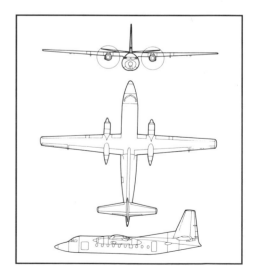

F.27 Mk 200 Friendship

ANTONOV An-22 ANTHEUS 'COCK' (U.S.S.R.)

AN-22 'Cock'

CCCP-46191

In its time the An-22 Antei (Antheus) was the world's largest aircraft although now beaten by the turbofan and 73.3 m (240.5 ft) span An-124 and 88.4 m (290 ft) An-225. An-22 was designed for the twin tasks of military heavy transport and support for the resources exploitation industry in Siberia (flying typically in civil Aeroflot markings). The specification for the type was issued in 1962, and the first example flew in February 1965. The type was first revealed in the West, where it had the NATO reporting name 'Cock' during the Paris air show of June 1965. At that time it was reported that the design could also be developed as a 724-passenger airliner, but this proposal came to nothing. Given the type's highly specialized role and size, it is not surprising that production was limited to only about 60 aircraft, all completed by 1974 and many still flying.

Keynotes of the design are four potent turboprops driving immense contra-rotating propeller units, and an upswept tail unit with twin vertical surfaces at about three-fifths span. The 14-wheel landing gear allows operations into and out of semi-prepared airstrips, and comprises a twin-wheel nose unit and two six-wheel units as main units; the latter are three twin-wheel units in each of the two lateral sponson fairings that provide an unobstructed hold. The upswept tail allows in the rear-fuselage a hydraulically operated ramp/door arrangement for the straight-in loading of items as large as tanks or complete missiles. The hold is 32.7 m (107 ft 3 in) long and 4.4 m (14 ft 5 in) wide and high, and has four overhead travelling gantries as well as two 2500-kg (5,511-lb) capacity winches for the loading of freight.

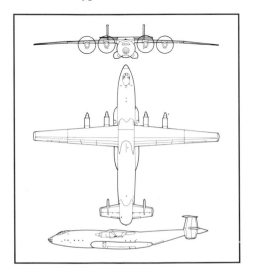

Antonov An-22 'Cock'

ANTONOV An-22 ANTHEUS 'COCK'
Role: Long-range freight transport
Crew/Accommodation: Five, plus up to 29 passengers/troops in upper cabin
Power Plant: Four 14,805 shp Kuznetsov NK 12MA turboprops
Dimensions: Span 64.4 .m (211.29 ft); length 57.31 m (188 ft); wing area 345 m² (3,713.6 sq ft)
Weights: Empty 118,727 kg (261,748 lb); MTOW 225,000 kg (496,040 lb)
Performance: Cruise speed 580 km/h (360 mph); operational ceiling 10,000 m (32,808 ft); range 5,000 km (2,698 naut. miles) with maximum payload
Load: Up to 60,000 kg (132,340 lb)

An Antonov An-22 of the Soviet civil operator Aeroflot

EMBRAER EMB-110 BANDEIRANTE Family (Brazil)

The Empresa Brasileira de Aeronáutica SA was created in 1969 to promote the development of an indigenous Brazilian aircraft industry, and began operation in January 1970. The company has had astonishing international success, particularly with a number of interesting light transports that most recently include the ERJ 135 and 145 regional turbofan jets. Early success came with the EMB-110 Bandeirante (pioneer), whose design origins lie in the period before EMBRAER's creation. The EMB-110

was evolved under the leadership of Max Holste as a utility light transport to meet the multi-role requirements of the Brazilian ministry of aeronautics, and first flew in October 1968 in the form of a YC-95 prototype.

The Bandeirante is of all-metal construction and of typical light transport configuration with low-set cantilever wings, a conventional fuselage and tail unit, retractable tricycle landing gear, and two wing-mounted Pratt & Whitney Canada PT6A turboprop engines. The

accommodation varies with model and role, but the EMB-110P2 is typical of the series with seating for 18–19 passengers. The type has been produced in a number of civil variants such as the 15-passenger EMB-110C feederliner, 7-passenger executive EMB-110E, all-cargo EMB-110K1, 18-passenger EMB-110P export model, a higher-capacity model with a fuselage stretch of 0.85 m (2 ft 9.5 in) in EMB-110P1 mixed or all-cargo and EMB-110P2 passenger subvariants, and the EMB-110P/41 higher-weight model in EMB-110P1/41 quick-change and EMB-110P2/41 passenger

subvariants. The EMB-110P2A accommodates 21 passengers. Large-scale production for the Brazilian Air Force resulted in a number of C-95 utility transport, R-95 survey and SC-95 transport and search-and-rescue models. Also produced was the EMB-111 Patrulha coastal patrol version operated as the P-95 with search radar, a tactical navigation system, wingtip tanks and provision for underwing weapons. Bandeirante production ended in 1994.

EMBRAER EMB-111 Patrulha

EMBRAER EMB-110P1A BANDEIRANTE
Role: Short-range passenger/cargo transport
Crew/Accommodation: Two, plus up to 19 passengers
Power Plant: Two 750 shp Pratt & Whitney PT6A-34 turboprops
Dimensions: Span 15.32 m (50.26 ft); length 15.08 m (49.47 ft); wing area 29.1 m² (313 sq ft)
Weights: Empty 3,630 kg (8,010 lb); MTOW 5,900 kg (13,010 lb)
Performance: Cruise speed 417 km/h (259 mph); operational ceiling up to 6,860 m (22,500 ft); range 1,898 km (1,179 miles)
Load: Up to 1,565 kg (3,450 lb) passenger version, or 1,724 kg (3,800 lb) cargo-carrier

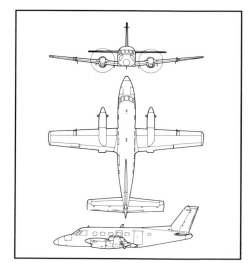

EMB-110 Bandeirante

CASA C-212 AVIOCAR (Spain)

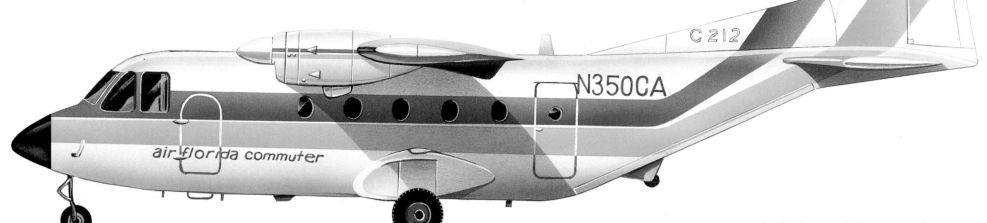

C-212 Aviocar

This simple yet effective light transport aircraft was developed to replace the Spanish Air Force's miscellany of obsolete transports. CASA conceived the type with the civil as well as military markets in mind, and thus schemed the type with STOL capability, highly cost-effective operation, great reliability, and simple maintenance. The resulting Aviocar is of all-metal construction and of typical airlifter configuration with an upswept tail unit above a rear ramp/door that provides straight-in access to the rectangular-section cabin; in the latest C-212 Series 300/400 forms, the cabin is 7.275 m (23.88 ft) long in passenger layout and 6.55 m (21.5 ft) in cargo layout, with a width at the floor of 2.1 m (6.92 ft) and 1.87 m (6.17 ft) respectively, and 1.8m (5.92 ft high.

The tricycle landing gear is fixed, and the attachment of the main units to external fairings leaves the hold entirely unobstructed.

The first C-212 first flew in March 1971, and it soon became clear that CASA had designed the right type as orders arrived from third-world civil operators as well as air forces. Spanish production has been complemented by Indonesian construction by IPTN.

More than 460 have been ordered of all versions, going to over 50 civil operators plus military/government agencies in 24 countries. Until recently the Series 300 Aviocar was the current production version, the last with all electro-mechanical instrumentation. For the latest Series 400, first flown in 1997, display screens provided a 'glass cockpit' environment. The military version is designated C-212M, while specialized variants for maritime patrol, anti-submarine, counter-insurgency, search and rescue, electronic warfare and other missions carry the designations 'MP', 'ASW' and 'DE Patrullero'.

C-212 Aviocar

CASA C-212 AVIOCAR Series 400, unless stated
Role: Short, rough field-going utility transport
Crew/Accommodation: Two, plus up to 2–6 passengers
Power Plant: Two 900 shp AlliedSignal TPE331-10R-513C turboprops for Series 300 and two 925 shp TPE331-12JR-701Cs for Series 400
Dimensions: Span 20.275 m (66.5 ft); length 16.154 m (53 ft); wing area 41 m² (441.3 sq ft)
Weights: Empty 3,780 kg (8.333 lb) for Series 300; MTOW 8,100 kg (17,857 lb)
Performance: Cruise speed 361 km/h (225 mph) at 3,050 m (10,000 ft); operational ceiling 7,925 m (26,000 ft); range 1,594 km (990 miles)
Load: Up to 2,320 kg (5,115 lb) of passengers or 2,800 kg (6,172 lb) of cargo for Series 300, 2,950 kg (6,504 lb) for Series 400

CASA C-212M Aviocar in military form with Angola

SHORTS 360 (United Kingdom)

Shorts 360

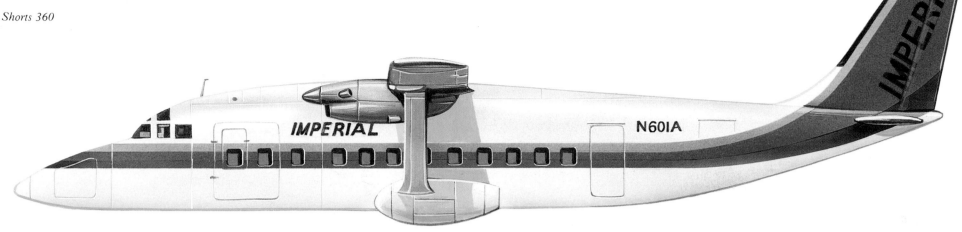

After the success of its SC.7 Skyvan series, Shorts decided to produce a larger and more refined derivative as the SD3-30 that then became the Shorts 330 with retractable tricycle landing gear and accommodation for 30 passengers. The type entered service in August 1976, and has proved most successful. Even so, the company appreciated that a larger-capacity type would broaden the series' market appeal, and the result was the Shorts 360. Market research indicated that capacity 20 per cent greater than that of the Shorts 330 was really desirable, and it was in 36-passenger configuration that the first Shorts 360 flew in June 1981 on the power of two 990-kW (1,327-shp) Pratt & Whitney Canada PT6A-65R turboprops.

The Shorts 360 is similar to its predecessor in being a high-wing monoplane with aerofoil-section lifting struts that brace the high aspect ratio wing to the sponsons that accommodate the main units of the retractable tricycle landing gear, but differs in having a single vertical tail in place of twin endplate surfaces, the lengthening of the forward fuselage by 0.91 m (3 ft 0 in) to allow the incorporation of an extra three-seat passenger row, and revision of the rear fuselage to improve aerodynamic form and permit the addition of another extra three-seat passenger row.

The Shorts 360 entered service in December 1982, and the type's only major improvement to date has been the introduction from 1986 of 1063-kW (1,424-shp) PT6A-65AR engines to produce the Shorts 360 Advanced. The maximum passenger payload is 3184 kg (7,020 lb), but in the type's alternative freight configuration the payload is somewhat increased to 3765 kg (8,300 lb).

Shorts 360

SHORTS 360-300
Role: Short range passenger transport/freighter
Crew/Accommodation: Two and two cabin crew, plus up to 37 passengers
Power Plant: Two 1,424 shp Pratt & Whitney Canada PT6A-67R turboprops
Dimensions: Span 22.80 m (74.79 ft); length 21.58 m (70.94 ft); wing area 42.18 m² (454.00 sq ft)
Weights: Empty 7,870 kg (17,350 lb); MTOW 12,292 kg (27,100 lb)
Performance: Maximum speed 401 km/h (216 knots) at 3,048 m (10,000 ft); operational ceiling 3,930 m (12,900 ft); range 1,178 km (732 miles) with 36 passengers
Load: Up to 4,536 kg (10,000 lb) for freighter version.
Note: operational ceiling artificially restricted for passenger comfort

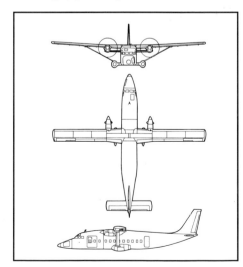

A Shorts 360-300

Caravan I

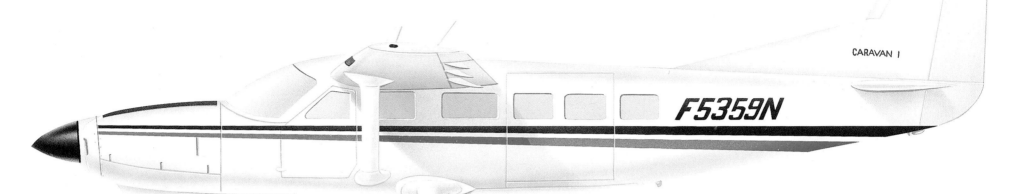

CARAVAN 1

F5359N

The Model 208 Caravan can be considered as Cessna's replacement for the elderly Model 185 Skywagon in the light utility transport role. The Model 208 offers its operators considerably greater capacity and performance, combined with more advanced features such as tricycle landing gear and the turboprop powerplant that runs off fuel that can be obtained anywhere in the world and also offers great reliability and better operating economics.

The first Model 208 flew in December 1982, and the first deliveries of production aircraft followed in 1985. The type can operate on sturdy wheeled or float landing gear, and is otherwise a conventional high-wing monoplane with a fuselage of slightly odd appearance because it has been optimized for the freight role in its long parallel upper and lower lines and large loading door in the side at easy loading/unloading height.

Current versions are the basic Caravan with a PT6A-114 engine, a cabin volume of 7.19 m³ (254 cu ft) plus optional 2.37 m³ (82.7 cu ft) external cargo pod, and with maximum seating for 14 persons; Caravan Floatplane, without external cargo pod but with baggage capacity in floats; the large Grand Caravan with a 675 shp PT6A-114A engine and cabin volume of 9.63 m³ (340 cu ft) plus a 3.16 m³ (111.5 cu ft) cargo pod; and Super Cargomaster, a cargo version of Grand Caravan. There is also a U-27A military version for U.S. foreign military sales programme.

Cessna Caravan I

CESNA GRAND CARAVAN
Role: Commercial and military short field-capable utility transport
Crew/Accommodation: One, plus up to 14 passengers
Power Plant: One 675 shp Pratt & Whitney Canada PT6A-114A turboprop
Dimensions: Span 15.88 m (52.08 ft); length 12.67 m (41.58 ft); wing area 25.96 m² (279.4 sq ft)
Weights: Empty 2,064 kg (4,550 lb); MTOW 3,856 kg (8,500 lb)
Performance: Cruise speed 324 km/h (202 mph) at 3,050 m (10,000 ft); operational ceiling 8,780 m (28,800 ft); range 1,783 km (1,109 miles)
Load: 1,921 kg (4,235 lb) useful load

A Cessna Caravan I of the small-package carrier Federal Express

SAAB 340 and 2000 (Sweden)

Saab 340

In January 1980, Saab and Fairchild agreed to undertake the collaborative design and development of a turboprop-powered small transport for the civil market. This was initially known as the Saab-Fairchild SF-340 and planned in the form of a low-wing monoplane featuring a wing of high aspect ratio with long-span slotted flaps and retractable tricycle landing gear with twin wheels on each unit. Construction is of the all-metal type, with selective use of composite materials in some areas, and while Saab was responsible for the fuselage, assembly and flight testing, Fairchild built the wings, tail unit and nacelles. The type was planned as a passenger transport with provision for 34 passengers in addition to a flight crew of two or three plus one flight attendant, but the cabin was schemed from the beginning for easy completion in the passenger/freight or alternative 16-passenger executive/corporate transport roles.

The first machine flew in January 1983 with 1215-kW (1,630-hp) General Electric CT7-5A turboprops, and the certification programme was undertaken by the first production machine in addition to the two prototypes. Certification was achieved in May 1984, and the type entered service in the following month. In November 1985, Fairchild indicated its unwillingness to continue with the programme, which thereupon became a Saab responsibility. Fairchild continued as a subcontractor until 1987, giving Saab time to complete additional construction facilities in Sweden. Early aircraft were limited to a maximum take-off weight of 11,794 kg (26,000 lb). Later machines were given CT7-5A2 turboprops driving larger-diameter propellers, and were cleared for higher weights. Since 1994 the standard version has been the 340B Plus (replacing the 340B of 1989–94 deliveries, which in turn had replaced the 340A). Production was expected to end in 1999, along with production of the 50–58-seat Saab 2000 (first flown in 1992).

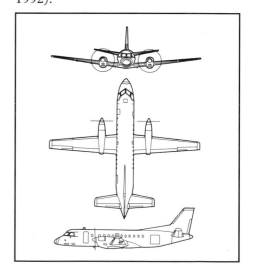

Saab 340

SAAB 340B Plus

Role: Regional passenger transport
Crew/Accommodation: Two and one cabin crew, plus up to 37 passengers
Power Plant: Two 1,870 shp General Electric CT7-9B turboprops
Dimensions: Span 21.44 m (70.33 ft); length 19.73 m (64.75 ft); wing area 41.81 m² (450.00 sq ft)
Weights: Empty 8,255 kg (18,135 lb); MTOW 13,155 kg (29,000 lb)
Performance: Typical cruise speed 528 km/h (328 mph); operational ceiling 7,620 m (25,000 ft); range 1,551 km (964 miles) with 35 passengers
Load: Up to 3,795 kg (8,366 lb)

A Saab 340 of the American operator Northwest Airlines

BOMBARDIER de HAVILLAND DASH 8Q (Canada)

Bombardier de Havilland Dash 8Q Series 100

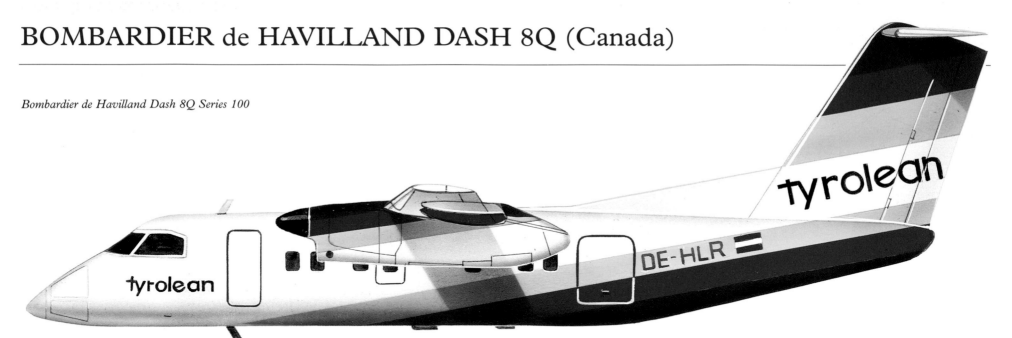

The DHC-8 was developed to the same basic operating philosophy as the 50-passenger DHC-7, but was sized for 40 passengers in the commuterliner role. As with other de Havilland Canada transports, STOL capability was a primary consideration, and the type was made attractive to potential operators by its fuel-economical turboprop engines driving propellers of large diameter, which turn slowly and so generate considerably less noise than fast-turning propellers of smaller diameter. Other features include a large cargo-loading door in the port side of the fuselage aft of the wing, retractable tricycle landing gear with twin-wheel main units, and a T-tail keeping the tailplane well clear of the disturbed airflow behind the wings and propellers.

The first of four pre-production aircraft flew in June 1983. The type entered revenue-earning service in December 1984. The baseline variant is now the Dash 8Q Series 100A with 2,000-shp Pratt & Whitney Canada PW120A turboprops. In its basic commuterliner layout, this carries a crew of three (two flight crew and one cabin attendant) and between 37–39 passengers. The same seating capacities apply to the Series 100B (PW121 engines) and Series 200A and B (PW123 series engines), all engines being of 2,150 shp rating. Seating jumps to 50–56 for the Series 300A, B and E, whose PW123 series engines are rated at 2,380 shp, 2,500 shp and 2,380 shp respectively. With these versions, the fuselage length increases to 25.68 m (84,25 ft). The largest versions are the Series 400A and B with 5,071 shp PW150A engines, 32.84 m (107.75 ft) length fuselages and seating for 70 and 72–78 passengers respectively.

Bombardier de Havilland Dash 8Q

---

de HAVILLAND CANADA DASH 8Q Series 100A

Role: Short field-capable passenger transport

Crew/Accommodation: Two, plus up to 39 passengers

Power Plant: Two 2,000 shp Pratt & Whitney Canada PW120A turboprops

Dimensions: Span 25.91 m (85 ft); length 22.25 m (73 ft); wing area 54.4 m² (585 sq ft)

Weights: Empty 10,310 kg (22,730 lb); MTOW 15,649 kg (34,500 lb)

Performance: Cruise speed 491 km/h (303 mph); operational ceiling 7,620 m (25,000 ft); range 1,365 km (848 miles)

Load: Up to 3,887 kg (8,570 lb)

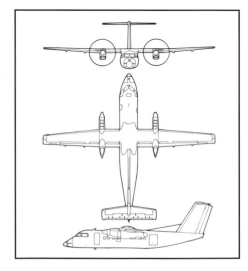

Bombardier de Havilland Dash 8Q

EMBRAER EMB-120 BRASILIA (Brazil)

EMB-120 Brasilia

The Brazilian government and EMBRAER were both highly encouraged by the EMB-110's penetration of the world market for commuterliners and feederliners. From this success, there emerged plans for an EMB-12X series of three pressurized types sharing a fuselage of common diameter but different lengths. Of these only the EMB-121 Xingu business transport actually

entered production. In September 1979 EMBRAER decided to move a step further up the size ladder with a pressurized 30-seat regional airliner, and this retained the overall configuration of the earlier 20-passenger EMB-120 Araguaia.

The type was designated EMB-120 and later named Brasilia, and metal was cut for the first aircraft in May 1981. Six aircraft were produced for the test and certification programmes, and the first machine flew in July 1983 as a low-wing monoplane with a circular-section fuselage, a T-tail, retractable tricycle landing gear, and a

powerplant of two wing-mounted 1118-kW (1,500-shp) Pratt & Whitney Canada PW115 turboprop engines. Though designed as a regional airliner with 30 seats, the Brasilia has a large cargo door in the port side of the rear fuselage, and is also available in freight and mixed-traffic versions, the former offering a payload of 3470-kg (7,650-lb) and the latter the capacity for 26 passengers

and 900-kg (1,984-lb) of cargo. The Brasilia has an airstair door on the port side of the forward fuselage to reduce demand on external support at small airports, and for the same reason is also offered with a Garrett auxiliary power unit in the tail cone as an option. Later aircraft are powered by a pair of 1343-kW (1,800-shp) PW118 turboprops for improved performance at higher weights.

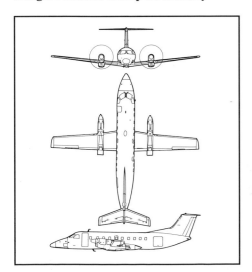

EMB-120 Brasilia

EMBRAER EMB-120 BRASILIA
Role: Short range passenger transport
Crew/Accommodation: Two and one cabin crew, plus up to 30 passengers
Power Plant: Two 1,600 shp Pratt & Whitney PW115 turboprops
Dimensions: Span 19.78 m (64.90 ft); length 20.00 m (65.62 ft); wing area 39.43 m² (424.42 sq ft)
Weights: Empty 6,878 kg (15,163 lb); MTOW 11,500 kg (25,353 lb)
Performance: Maximum speed 556 km/h (300 knots) at 7,620 m (25,000 ft); operational ceiling 9,083 m (29,800 ft); range 1,751 km (945 naut. miles) with 30 passengers
Load: Up to 3,470 kg (7,650 lb)

An EMBRAER EMB-120 Brasilia of the German carrier DLT

Civil Jet-Engined Transports

The turboprop, turbojet and turbofan are related in that all are turbine engines and therefore 'jets'. Because of this, it is slightly misleading to title only this section as 'Jet'-engined transports, having separated out the propeller-driven aircraft. Yet, in the common usage of the term 'jet', most people think only of an engine without a propeller.

By the early years of World War II, several British companies were engaged in jet propulsion research, as were others abroad. In 1941 de Havilland began the design of what ultimately became the Goblin engine, used successfully on its Vampire fighter. The company also required a larger turbojet engine to power a proposed jet airliner, the engine and airliner eventually becoming the Ghost and Comet respectively. The Ghost adopted the same simple form of the smaller Goblin and Ghost 50 form was the first turbojet engine to obtain civil Type Approval. With Ghost 50s buried neatly into its wing roots, the de Havilland Comet first flew in 1949, gained it certificate of airworthiness in 1952 and entered commercial service later that year.

What was a British triumph soon turned to tragedy, however, when in March 1953 a Comet 1 on its delivery flight in stages to Australia crashed on take-off in Pakistan. Then, in May, a BOAC Comet 1 was lost near Calcutta, the first fatal accident for a turbojet airliner while on a scheduled service. British and foreign jetliner manufacturers learned from the tragedies.

While de Havilland developed and produced superior models of the Comet that later performed well in commercial use, Boeing had meantime flown the prototype of a jet which it had developed as a private venture against the perceived needs of the U.S.A.F. for a tanker/transport able to service present and future high-speed combat aircraft, while suiting commercial applications. This was known as the Model 367-80 and, in 1954, was ordered for the U.S.A.F. as the KC-135. Importantly, in July 1955 Boeing gained the necessary official clearance to permit production of the commercial variant as the Model 707, to be built simultaneously with the military KC-135. Backed by vast military orders and with many potential worldwide customers for its jetliner,

Boeing never looked back. Indeed, the last 707-based airframe did not leave the production line until 1992, although for the final decade production was at a low rate to satisfy only the need to provide airframes for specialized military aircraft. By then, of course, a wide range of Boeing jetliners had been created.

Despite early setbacks, Britain still managed to claim the first transatlantic passenger services using a turbojet airliner when BOAC inaugurated Comet 4 flights between London and New York in October 1958. However, the Boeing 707 was in a class of its own and in 1959 was used for the first trans-Pacific jetliner service and, in the hands of Pan-American World Airways, the first round-the-world passenger jetliner service. Turbojet airliners from France, the Soviet Union and elsewhere soon got in on the act, and it was the combined talent of France and Britain that a decade later went on to win the battle to produce a viable supersonic airliner against strong competition from the Soviet Union and to a lesser extent the U.S.A.

Today, in 1999, the vast majority of the world's larger airliners are built by just two companies, Boeing of the U.S.A. and the rival European Airbus Industrie. Boeing, having taken over McDonnell Douglas, has a very extensive range that spans from the smallest Model 717 to the huge Model 747 and includes the extremely important C-17 Globemaster III military transport, whereas Airbus will soon add the new A3XX to its list of highly successful products, to be the world's first ultra-large, full double-deck, long-range airliner.

RIGHT
Impression of the Airbus A3XX ultra-large airliner for service in the 21st century

de HAVILLAND D.H.106 COMET (United Kingdom)

D.H.106 Comet 4

The Comet was the world's first turbojet-powered airliner, but failed to secure the financial advantages of this potentially world-beating lead because of technical problems. The type was planned from 1944 in response to the far-sighted Type IV specification resulting from the Brabazon Committee's wartime deliberations into the shape of British air transport needs after the end of World War II. It

first flew in July 1949 with four de Havilland Ghost 50 centrifugal-flow turbojets. The type entered service in January 1952 as the Comet 1 with multi-wheel bogies rather than the two prototypes' single wheels on the main landing gear units. The Comet 1 was used initially as a freighter, and only later as a passenger-carrying airliner, and deliveries to the British Overseas Airways Corporation totalled nine between January 1951 and September 1952; there followed 10 Comet 1As with greater fuel capacity.

One crash in 1953 and two in 1954 resulted in the type's grounding, and it

was then established that fatigue failures at the corners of the rectangular window frames were to blame. Rounded windows were introduced on the 44-passenger Comet 2, of which 12 were built with a 0.91-m (3-ft) fuselage stretch and axial-flow Rolls-Royce Avon 503 engines, but these BOAC aircraft were diverted to the RAF as 70-passenger Comet C.Mk 2s. The Comet 3 was precursor to a transatlantic version

that entered service as the 78-seat Comet 4 with Avon 524 engines in May 1958, when the conceptually more advanced Boeing Model 707 and Douglas DC-8 were already coming to the fore of the market. Some 27 were built. Derivatives were the 18 shorter-range Comet 4Bs with a shorter wing but longer fuselage for 99 passengers, and the 29 Comet 4Cs combining the wing of the Comet 4 with the Comet 4B's fuselage.

de Havilland D.H.106 Comet 4

de HAVILLAND D.H. 106 COMET 4
Role: Intermediate range passenger transport
Crew/Accommodation: Three, plus four cabin crew and up to 78 passengers
Power Plant: Four 4,649 kgp (10,250 lb s.t.) Rolls-Royce Avon RA29 turbojets
Dimensions: Span 35 m (114.83 ft); length 33.99 m (111.5 ft); wing area 197 m² (2,121 sq ft)
Weights: Empty 34,200 kg (75,400 lb); MTOW 72,575 kg (160,000 lb)
Performance: Cruise speed 809 km/h (503 mph) at 12,802 m (42,000 ft); operational ceiling 13,411+ m (44,000+ ft); range 5,190 km (3,225 miles) with full load
Load: Up to 9,206 kg (20,286 lb)

This is a Comet 4B of British European Airways

BOEING 707 and 720 (U.S.A.)

Boeing 707-300C

Though preceded into service by the de Havilland Comet, the Model 707 must rightly be regarded as the world's first effective long-range jet transport. In an exceptionally bold technical and commercial move, Boeing decided during August 1952 to develop, as a private venture, the prototype of an advanced transport with military as well as civil applications. This Model 367-80 prototype first flew in July 1954 with 4309-kg (9,500-lb) thrust Pratt &

Whitney JT3P turbojets, and in October of the same year the company's faith in its capabilities was rewarded by the first of many orders for the KC-135A inflight refuelling tanker derived from the 'Dash 80'. Once the U.S. Air Force had given clearance, the company then started marketing the type as the 707 civil transport with a slightly wider fuselage, and in October 1955 Pan American took the bold step of ordering the 707 for its long-haul domestic network in the United States.

A total of 1,010 707s and closely related 720s was built, in the last decade (1982–92), however, only as airframes for military special versions, while U.S.A.F. KC-135s and C-135/137s were delivered during 1957-66 (808 aircraft) plus 12 to France. The major commercial variants were the Model 707-120 transcontinental airliner with 6123-kg (13,500-lb) thrust Pratt & Whitney JT3C turbojets, the Model 707-120B with JT3D turbofans, the Model 707-220 with 7938-kg (17,500-lb) thrust JT4A turbojets, the Model 707-320 intercontinental airliner with longer wing and fuselage plus 7938-kg

(17,500-lb thrust JT4A turbojets, the Model 707-320B with aerodynamic refinements and turbofans, the Model 707-320C convertible or freighter variants with turbofans, and the Model 707-420 with 7983-kg (17,600-lb) thrust Rolls-Royce Conway turbofans. The model 720 was aerodynamically similar to the Model 707-120 but had a shorter fuselage plus a new and lighter structure optimized for the intermediate-range role. There was also a Model 720B turbofan-powered variant.

A Boeing 707-320 of Air India

BOEING 707-320C
Role: Long-range passenger/cargo transport
Crew/Accommodation: Three, plus five/six cabin crew, plus up to 189 passengers
Power Plant: Four 8,618 kgp (19,000 lb s.t.) Pratt & Whitney JT3D-7 turbofans
Dimensions: Span 44.42 m (145.71 ft); length 45.6 m (152.92 ft); wing area 283.4 m² (3050 sq ft)
Weights: Empty 66,224 kg (146,000 lb); MTOW 151,315 kg (333,600 lb)
Performance: Cruise speed 886 km/h (550 mph) at 8,534 m (28,000 ft); operational ceiling 11,885 m (39,000 ft); range 6,920 km (4,300 miles) with maximum payload
Load: Up to 41,453 kg (91,390 lb)

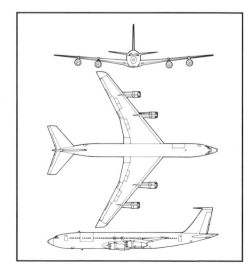

Boeing 707-300C

SUD-EST CARAVELLE (France)

Caravelle VI-N

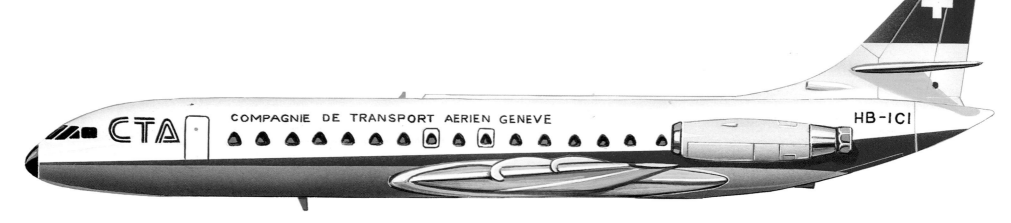

The Caravelle was France's first jet-powered airliner, the world's first short/medium-range jet airliner, and also the world's first airliner with its engines pod-mounted on the sides of the rear fuselage. The type resulted from a 1951 French civil aviation ministry requirement, and out of submissions from six manufacturers the S.E.210 was selected for hardware development in the form of two prototypes. The first of these flew in May 1955 with two 4536-kg (10,000-lb) thrust Rolls-Royce Avon RA.26 turbojets and had accommodation for 52 passengers.

Successful evaluation paved the way for the Caravelle I with its fuselage lengthened by 1.41 m (4 ft 7.5 in) for 64 passengers. The 19 Caravelle Is had 4763-kg (10,500-lb) Avon RA. 29 Mk 522s, while the 13 Caravelle IAs had Avon RA.29/1 Mk 526s. Next came 78 Caravelle IIIs with 5307-kg (11,700-lb) thrust Avon RA.29/3 Mk 527s, and all but one of the Mk I aircraft were upgraded to this standard. The Caravelle VI followed in two forms: the 53 VI-Ns had 5534-kg (12,200-lb) Avon RA.29/6 Mk 531s and the 56 VI-Rs had thrust-reversing 5715-kg (12,600-lb) thrust Avon Mk 532R or 533R engines.

Considerable refinement went into the Super Caravelle 10B, of which 22 were built. This first flew in March 1964 with extended wing roots, double-slotted flaps, a larger tailplane, a lengthened fuselage for 104 passengers, and 6350-kg (14,000-lb) thrust Pratt & Whitney JT8D-7 turbofans. The 20 Super Caravelle 10Rs used the Mk VI airframe with JT8D-7 engines, and 20 were built. The final models were the six Caravelle IIRs for mixed freight and passenger operations, and the 12 Caravelle 12s lengthened for 140-passenger accommodation and powered by 6577-kg (14,500-lb) thrust JT8D-9s.

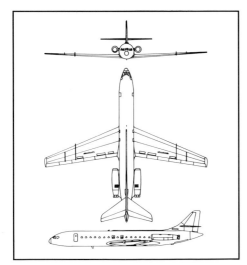

Caravelle

AEROSPATIALE (SUD AVIATION) CARAVELLE 12

Role: Short-range passenger transport
Crew/Accommodation: Two, four cabin crew, plus up to 140 passengers
Power Plant: Two 6,577 kgp (14,500 lb s.t.) Pratt & Whitney JT8D-9 turbofans
Dimensions: Span 34.30 m (112.5 ft); length 36.24 m (118.75 ft); wing area 146.7 m² (1,579 sq ft)
Weights: Empty 31,800 kg (70,107 lb); MTOW 56,699 kg (125,000 lb)
Performance: Maximum speed 785 km/h (424 knots) at 7,620 m (25,000 ft); operational ceiling 12,192 m (40,000+ ft); range 1,870 km (1,162 miles) with full payload
Load: Up to 13,200 kg (29,101 lb)

Caravelle VI-N

DOUGLAS DC-8 (U.S.A.)

Douglas DC-8-50

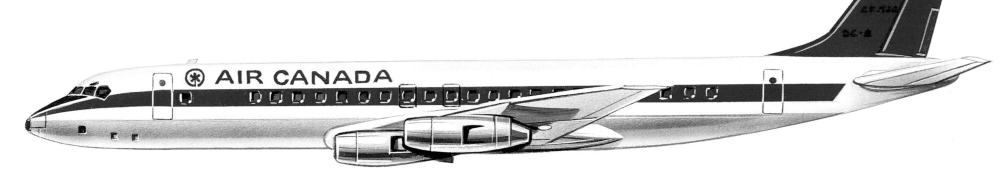

After planning the DC-7D with four 4273-kW (5,730-shp) Rolls-Royce Tyne turboprop engines, Douglas decided instead to challenge the Boeing Model 707 in the market for turbojet-powered airliners. The result was the DC-8, a worthy type that nevertheless trailed the Model 707 because of its later start and the availability of only a single fuselage length. In an effort to catch up with the Model 707, Douglas produced nine test aircraft with three different types of engine, and the first of these

flew in May 1958. Total production of the initial five series was 294 built over a period of nine years. These series were the DC-8-10 domestic model with 6123-kg (13,500-lb) thrust Pratt & Whitney JT3C-6 turbojets, the similar DC-8-20 with uprated engines for 'hot-and-high' routes, the DC-8-30 intercontinental model typically with 7620-kg (16,800-lb) thrust JT4A-9 turbojets, the similar DC-8-40 with 7938-kg (17,500-lb) thrust Rolls-Royce Conway Mk 509 turbofans, and the DC-8-50 with Pratt &

Whitney JT3D turbofans and a rearranged cabin for 189 passengers. The DC-8F Jet Trader was based on the DC-8-50 but available in all-freight or convertible freight/passenger layouts.

From 1967 production was of the JT3D-powered Super Sixty series, of which 262 were produced. This series comprised the DC-8 Super 61 with the fuselage stretched by 11.18 m (36 ft 8 in) for 259 passengers, the DC-8 Super 62 with span increased by 1.83 m (6 ft 0 in) and length by 2.03 m (6 ft 8 in) for 189 passengers carried over very long range, and the DC-8 Super

63 combining the Super 61's fuselage and Super 62's wing. These models could be delivered in all-passenger, all-freight, or convertible freight/passenger configurations. Finally came the Super Seventy series, which comprised Super 61, 62, and 63 aircraft converted with General Electric/SNECMA CFM56 turbofans with the designations DC-8 Super 71, 72, and 73 respectively.

A Douglas DC-8-50 of Japan Air Lines

DOUGLAS DC-8-63
Role: Long-range passenger transport
Crew/Accommodation: Four and four cabin crew, plus up to 251 passengers
Power Plant: Four 8,618 kgp (19,000 lb s.t.) Pratt & Whitney JT3D-7 turbofans
Dimensions: Span 45.24 m (148.42 ft); length 57.1 m (187 ft); wing area 271.93 m² (2,927 sq ft)
Weights: Empty 71,401 kg (157,409 lb); MTOW 158,760 kg (350,000 lb)
Performance: Cruise speed 959 km/h (517 knots) at 10,973 m (36,000 ft); operational ceiling 12,802 m (42,000 ft); range 6,301 km (3,400 naut. miles) with full payload
Load: Up to 30,126 kg (55,415 lb)

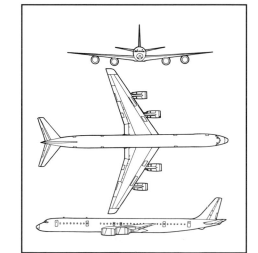

Douglas DC-8 Series 70

VICKERS VC10 (United Kingdom)

Vickers VC10

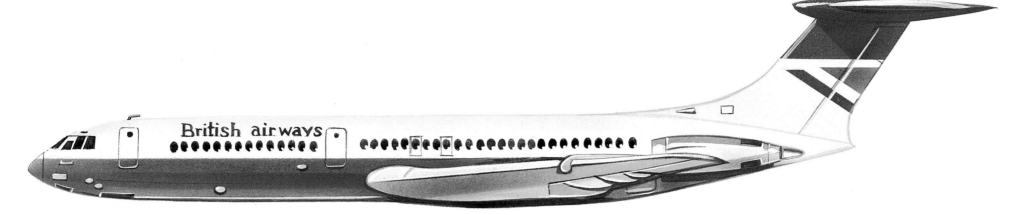

In 1957, the British Overseas Airways Corporation issued a requirement for an airliner able to carry a 15,422-kg (34,000-lb) payload over a range of 6437 km (4,000 miles) on the operator's Commonwealth routes. Vickers responded with its Type 1100 design. This was optimized for BOAC's route network, which included many 'hot-and-high' airports with short runways, with a large wing

left uncluttered for its primary lifting task by the location of the four engines in paired pods on the sides of the rear fuselage below the tall T-tail. Other features were the retractable tricycle landing gear and six-abreast seating in the pressurized circular-section fuselage.

The first VC10 flew in July 1962, and the type entered service with BOAC in April 1964 with 9525-kg (21,000-lb) thrust Rolls-Royce Conway RCo. 42 turbofans, a crew of 10 and a payload of between 115 and 135 passengers. BOAC took 12 such

aircraft, and other customers were Ghana Airways (two), British United Airways (three), and the Royal Air Force (14 VC10 C.Mk 1s with a revised wing, greater fuel capacity and Conway RCo.43 engines). The prototype was also revised to production standard and was then sold to Laker Airways.

Development evolved the Type 1150 that entered production as the Super VC10 with Conway RCo.43 engines, greater fuel capacity and a fuselage lengthened by 3.96 m (13 ft 0 in). BOAC took 17 such aircraft and

East African Airways another five. Because of its large wing, the VC10 had inferior operating economics to the Boeing Model 707, and most airports upgraded their facilities to cater for the Model 707 and Douglas DC-8.

The RAF bought from airlines VC10s and Super VC10s for conversion as VC10 K.Mks 2, 3 and 4 inflight refuelling tankers (14 aircraft). Many VC10 C.Mk 1s were also adapted as two-point tanker transports with the designation VC10 C.Mk1(K).

Vickers VC10 K.Mk 3

VICKERS/BRITISH AIRCRAFT CORPORATION SUPER VC-10
Role: Long range passenger transport
Crew/Accommodation: Five and seven cabin crew, plus up to 180 passengers
Power Plant: Four 9,888 kgp (21,800 lb) Rolls-Royce Conway RC0.43D Mk 550 turbofans
Dimensions: Span 44.55 m (146.17 ft); length 52.32 m (171.66 ft); wing area 272.40 m² (2,932 sq ft)
Weights: Empty 71,940 kg (158,594 lb); MTOW 151,950 kg (335,000 lb)
Performance: Maximum speed 935 km/h (505 knots) at 9,449 m (31,000 ft); operational ceiling 11,582 m (38,000 ft); range 7,596 km (4,720 miles) with full payload
Load: Up to 27,360 kg (60,321 lb)

A Vickers Super VC10 of East African Airways

BOEING 727 (U.S.A.)

Boeing Model 727-100

The Model 727 was conceived as a short/medium-range partner to the Model 707, with the primary task of bringing passengers to the larger airports used by the long-range type. The type was designed for as much construction commonality as possible with the Model 707, and among other features was designed to use the same fuselage cross-section. The design team considered 70 concepts before finalizing its concept for the Model

727 as a fairly radical type able to meet the apparently conflicting requirements for high cruising speed at the lowest possible altitude and minimum seat/mile costs. Other factors that had to be taken into account were frequent take-off/landing cycles, the need for fast 'turn-round' time, and the need for low take-off noise so that the type could use airports close to urban areas. The Model 727 emerged with three rear-

mounted engines, a T-tail and an uncluttered wing with triple-slotted flaps along its trailing edges. Independence of airport services was ensured by an auxiliary power unit and a ventral airstair/door.

The Model 727 first flew in February 1963, and production has reached 1,831 in two main variants. The basic variant is the Model 727-100, which was also produced in convertible and quick-change convertible derivatives. Then came the Model 727-200 lengthened by 6.1 m (20 ft) and featuring the structural modifications required for operation

at higher weights; the latest version is the Advanced 727-200 with a performance data computer system to improve operating economy and safety. Also operational in smaller numbers is the Model 727F, which was produced to the special order of small-package operator Federal Express; this variant has no fuselage windows and can carry 26,649-kg (58,750-lb) of freight.

A Boeing 727-200 of Pan American World Airways

BOEING 727-200
Role: Intermediate-range passenger transport
Crew/Accommodation: Three and four cabin crew, plus up to 189 passengers
Power Plant: Three 7,257 kgp (16,000 lb s.t.) Pratt & Whitney JT8D-17 turbofans
Dimensions: Span 32.9 m (108 ft); length 46.7 m (153.17 ft); wing area 153.3 m² (1,650 sq ft)
Weights: Empty 46,164 kg (101,773 lb); MTOW 95,028 kg (209,500 lb)
Performance: Cruise speed 982 km/h (530 knots) at 7,620 m (25,000 ft); operational ceiling 11,582+ m (38,000+ ft); range 5,371 km (2,900 naut. miles)
Load: Up to 18,597 kg (41,000 lb)

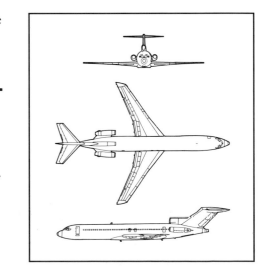

Boeing Model 727-200

BRITISH AIRCRAFT CORPORATION ONE-ELEVEN (United Kingdom)

BAC One-Eleven 500

This pioneering airliner was conceived as the Hunting H.107 short-range airliner with accommodation for 59 passengers, and to provide the type with excellent field performance and low cabin noise levels it was decided to use aft-mounted engines; this left the wing uncluttered and therefore better able to perform its primary function, and dictated the use of a T-tail to lift the tailplane well clear of the jet exhausts. Hunting was bought by

BAC and the H.107 became the BAC 107. There was little airline enthusiasm for an airliner with so small a passenger payload, and the basic concept was therefore enlarged to provide 79-passenger capacity. This was redesignated the BAC 111, and later the One-Eleven. The design was finalized with a circular-section pressurized fuselage with a ventral airstair let into the underside of the fuselage under the tail unit, a low-set wing of modest sweep with Fowler trailing-edge flaps, and a variable-incidence tailplane at the very top of the vertical tail surfaces.

The prototype flew in August 1963 with two 4722-kg (10,410-lb) thrust Rolls-Royce Spey Mk 506 turbofans, and was lost in a fatal crash some two months later as a result of a 'deep stall' occasioned by the aft engine/ T-tail configuration. After this problem had been cured, useful sales were secured for the basic One-Eleven Series 200 with Spey Mk 506s, the One-Eleven Mk 300 with 5171-kg (11,400-lb) thrust Spey Mk 511s, the generally similar but higher-weight

One-Eleven Mk 400 for U.S. airlines, the stretched One-Eleven Series 500 for 119 passengers, and the 'hot and high' One-Eleven Series 475 with the fuselage of the Series 400 plus the wings and powerplant of the Series 500. The One-Eleven production line was bought by Romaero in Romania where nine One-Elevens were built for a short time, the first Romaero 1-11 flying in 1982.

British Aircraft Corporation One-Eleven 675

BRITISH AIRCRAFT CORPORATION ONE-ELEVEN 500

Role: Short-range passenger transport
Crew/Accommodation: Two and three/four cabin crew, plus up to 119 passengers
Power Plant: Two 5,692 kgp (12,500 lb s.t.) Rolls-Royce Spey 512-DW turbofans
Dimensions: Span 28.5 m (92.5 ft); length 32.61 m (107 ft); wing area 95.78 m² (1,031 sq ft)
Weights: Empty 24,758 kg (54,582 lb); MTOW 47,000 kg (104,500 lb)
Performance: Maximum speed 871 km /h (470 knots) at 6,400 m (21,000 ft); range 2,380 km (1,480 miles) with full passenger load
Load: Up to 11,983 kg (26,418 lb) including belly cargo

The BAC One-Eleven pioneered the aft engine/T-tail combination

ILYUSHIN Il-62 (U.S.S.R.)

Il-62M

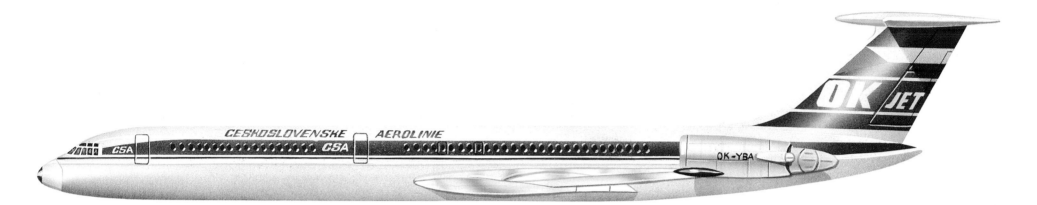

The Il-62 (known to NATO as 'Classic') was developed as a long-range airliner to complement and then to supplant the Tupolev Tu-114 on domestic and international routes. The Soviets specified high levels of comfort and performance in the hope that this would result in a type that would gain a measure of the export success that had eluded earlier Soviet airliners. The first Il-62 flew in January 1963 with four 7,500-kg (16,535-lb) thrust Lyulka AL-7 turbojets as the planned 10,500-kg (23,150-lb) thrust Kuznetsov NK-8-4

turbofans were not yet ready for flight. Clearly the design had been influenced by that of the Vickers VC10 in its configuration with a large wing, a T-tail, rear-mounted engines, and retractable tricycle landing gear. This similarity was also carried over into the flight test programme for, like the VC10, the Il-62 required lengthy development for the problem of its deep-stall tendency to be overcome. The NK-4 turbofans were introduced later in the test programme, which involved two prototypes and three pre-production aircraft.

The initial Il-62 production version entered service in September 1967 with accommodation for between 168 and 186 passengers, and cascade-type thrust reversers were fitted only on the outer engines. In 1971 there appeared the Il-62M with 11,000-kg (24,250-lb) thrust Soloviev D-30KU turbofans with clamshell-type thrust reversers, and the improved specific fuel consumption of this more advanced engine type combined with additional fuel capacity (a fuel tank in the fin) to improve the payload/range performance to a marked degree over

that of the Il-62. Other improvements were a revised flight deck, new avionics, and wing spoilers that could be operated differentially for roll control. The Il-62MK of 1978 introduced structure, landing gear and control system modifications to permit operations at higher weights. All production ended in the mid-1990s.

An Ilyushin Il-62 long-range airliner of Aeroflot

ILYUSHIN Il-62M 'CLASSIC'
Role: Long-range passenger transport
Crew/Accommodation: Five, four cabin crew, plus up to 186 passengers
Power Plant: Four 11,500 kgp (25,350 lb s.t.) Soloviev D-30KU turbofans
Dimensions: Span 43.2 m (141.75 ft); length 53.12 m (174.28 ft); wing area 279.6 m² (3,010 sq ft)
Weights: Empty 69,400 kg (153,000 lb); MTOW 165,000 kg (363,760 lb)
Performance: Cruise speed 900 km/h (485 knots) at 12,000 m (39,370 ft); operational ceiling 13,000+ m (42,650+ ft); range 8,000 km (4,317 naut. miles) with full payload
Load: Up to 23,000 kg (50,700 lb)

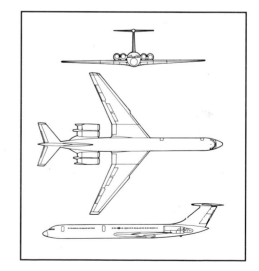

Ilyushin Il-62M

McDonnell Douglas MD-80

Planned as a medium-range partner to the DC-8, the DC-9 was then recast as a short-range type to compete with the BAC One-Eleven. Having learned the sales disadvantages of a single-length fuselage with the DC-8, Douglas planned the DC-9 with length options, and decided to optimize the efficiency of the wing by pod-mounting engines on the fuselage sides under a T-tail. The type first flew in February 1965 and built up an excellent sales record based on low operating costs and fuselage length tailored to customer requirements. The success of the type

also demanded so high a level of production investment, however, that Douglas was forced to merge with McDonnell.

The variants of the initial production series were the DC-9-10 with Pratt & Whitney JT8D turbofans and 90 passengers, the DC-9-15 with uprated engines, the DC-9-20 for 'hot-and-high' operations with more power and span increased by 1.22 m (4 ft 0 in), the DC-9-30 with the fuselage stretched by 4.54 m (14 ft 10.75 in) for 119 passengers, the DC-9-40 with a further stretch of 1.92 m (6 ft 3.5 in) for 132 passengers, and the DC-9-50 with more power and a further stretch of 2.44 m (8 ft 0 in) for 139 passengers. Developments for the military were the C-9A Nightingale aeromedical

transport based on the DC-9-30, and the C-9B Skytrain II fleet logistic transport combining features of the DC-9-30 and -40. Production totalled 976, and from 1975 McDonnell Douglas offered the DC-9 Super Eighty series with a longer fuselage and the refanned JT8D (-200 series) turbofan. This first flew in October 1979, and variants became the DC-9 Super 81 (now MD-81) with JT8D-209s and a fuselage stretched by 4.34 m (14ft 3 in) for 172 passengers, the DC-9 Super 82 (now MD-82) with JT8D-217s, the DC-9 Super 83 (now MD-83) with JT8D-219s and extra fuel, the DC-9 Super 87 (now MD-87) with JT8D-217Bs and a

fuselage shortened by 5.0 m (16 ft 5 in), and the DC-9 Super 88 (now MD-88) development of the MD-82 with JT8D-217Cs and an electronic flight instruments system combined with a flight-management computer and inertial navigation system. McDonnell also produced the MD-90 series, based on the MD-8C but with electronic engine controls, modernized flight deck, a fuselage lengthened to 46.51 m (152.6 ft), Internation Aero Engines turbofans and many other improvements. First flown in 1993, it is now also a Boeing type since the merger of Boeing and McDonnell Douglas.

McDonnell Douglas DC-9 Super 80

DOUGLAS DC-9-10
Role: Short-range passenger transport
Crew/Accommodation: Two and three cabin crew, plus up to 90 passengers
Power Plant: Two 6,580 kgp (14,500 lb s.t.) Pratt & Whitney JT8D-9 turbofans
Dimensions: Span 27.2 m (89.42 ft); length 31.8 m (104.42 ft); wing area 86.8 m² (934.3 sq ft)
Weights: Empty 23,060 kg (50,848 lb); MTOW 41,142 kg (90,700 lb)
Performance: Cruise speed 874 km/h (471 knots) at 9,144 m (30,000 ft); operational ceiling 12,497 m (41,000 ft); range 2,038 km (1,100 naut. miles) with maximum payload
Load: Up to 8,707 kg (19,200 lb)

A McDonnell Douglas MD-83

BOEING 737 (U.S.A.)

Boeing 737-200

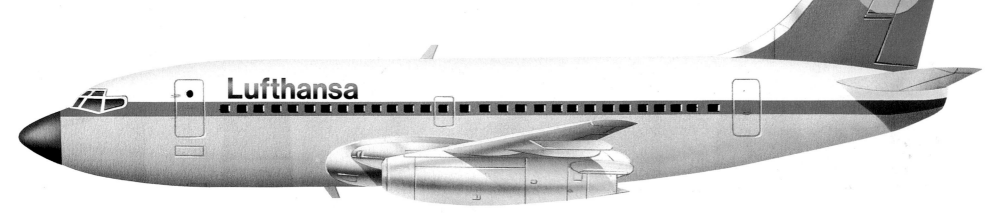

The short/medium range Model 737 became the small brother to the 707 and 727, and completed the Boeing family of airliners covering the full spectrum of commercial operations at the time of the company's November 1964 decision to design such a type. The Model 737 is currently the world's best-selling airliner, with more than 4,000 ordered. Originally intended for short sectors, the Model 737 first flew in April 1967. Despite the somewhat different appearance of

the two aircraft, Boeing managed about 60 per cent commonality of structure and systems between the Models 727 and 737.

The initial variant was the Model 737-100 for 100 passengers, but only a few were built before production switched to the larger 737-200 for 130 passengers, offering also convertible, quick-change convertible, and advanced derivatives. In 1984 came the 737-300 with an advanced technology flight deck, 9072-kg (20,000-lb) thrust

CFM56-3 turbofans (instead of the previous Pratt & Whitney JT8Ds) and further lengthening for 128–149 passengers, while in February 1988 the 737-400 flew offering up to 168 passengers in a 3.05-m (10-ft) longer fuselage, with the basic engine option of 9,980-kg (22,000-lb) CFM 56-35. The 737-500 for 108–132 passengers flew in June 1989, the basic engines derated to 8,391-kg (18,500-lb) thrust. Next generation versions are

the 108–140-passenger 737-600, 128–149-passenger 737-700, 162–189-passenger 737-800 and largest 737-900, offering CFM56-7B engines on larger wings. The 737-700 and -800 first flew in 1997.

Boeing 737-300s

BOEING 737-300
Role: Short/medium-range passenger transport
Crew/Accommodation: Two and four cabin crew, plus 149 passengers
Power Plant: Two 9,072 kgp (20,000 lb s.t.) CFM International CFM56-3B or 3C1 turbofans
Dimensions: Span 28.9 m (94.75 ft); length 33.4 m (109.58 ft); wing area 105.44 m² (1,135 sq ft)
Weights: Empty 32,704 kg (72,100 lb); MTOW 56,472 kg (124,500 lb)
Performance: Cruise speed 908 km/h (564 mph) at 7,925 m (26,000 ft); operational ceiling 11,278 m (37,000 ft); range 4,184 km (2,600 miles) with 124 passengers
Load: 16,030 kg (35,270 lb)

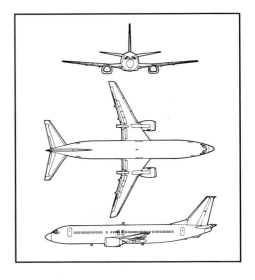

Boeing 737-400

FOKKER F.28 FELLOWSHIP and 100 (Netherlands)

F.28 Fellowship Mk 1000

The F.28 Fellowship was designed as a complement to the turboprop-powered F.27 with slightly higher passenger capacity and considerably improved performance through the use of a twin-turbofan powerplant. Initial design work began in 1960, and Fokker opted for a T-tail configuration and rear-mounted Rolls-Royce Spey engines to provide an uncluttered wing. The first of three F.28 prototypes flew in May 1967,

and the certification and delivery of the initial production machines were achieved at the same time in February 1969.

The first production version was the F.28 Mk 1000 for 65 passengers on two 4468-kg (9,850-lb) thrust Spey Mk 555-15s, and a subvariant was the F.28 MK 1000C with a large cargo door on the port side of the forward fuselage for all-freight or mixed freight/passenger services. Subsequent models have been the

F.28 Mk 2000 with its fuselage stretched by 2.21 m (7 ft 3 in) for 79 passengers, and the F.28 Mks 3000 and 4000 with the fuselages of the Mks 1000 and 2000 respectively, span increased by 1.57 m (6 ft 11.5 in), and two 4491-kg (9,900-lb) thrust Spey Mk 555-15Ps.

In order to keep the type matched to current airline demands, in November 1983 Fokker announced an updated and stretched Fokker 100 version. This was given a revised wing of greater efficiency and spanning

3.00 m (9 ft 9.5 in) more than that of the F.28, a larger tailplane, a fuselage stretched by 5.74 m (18 ft 10in) by plugs forward and aft of the wing to increase capacity to 107 passengers, and Rolls-Royce Tay 620-15 or Tay 650 turbofans. At the same time, the interior was completely remodelled, composite materials were introduced, and an electronic flight instrument system was introduced. The first Fokker 100 flew in November 1986, and 278 were delivered before production was brought to an end in 1997 following the company's bankruptcy.

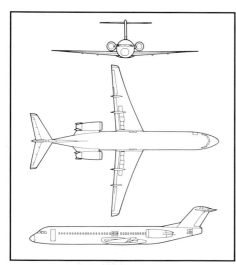

Fokker 100

FOKKER 100
Role: Short-range jet passenger transport
Crew/Accommodation: Two and four cabin crew, plus up to 109 passengers
Power Plant: Two 6,282 kgp (13,850 lb s.t.) Rolls-Royce Tay 620-15 or 6,850 kgp (15,100 lb s.t.) Tay 650 turbofans
Dimensions: Span 28.08 m (92.13 ft); length 35.53 m (116.57 ft); wing area 93.5 m² (1,006.5 sq ft)
Weights: Empty 24,593 kg (54,218 lb) with Tay 620s; MTOW 43,090 kg (95,000 lb) standard
Performance: Cruise speed 765 km/h (475 mph) at 8,534 m (28,000 ft); operational ceiling 10,668 m (35,000 ft); range 2,389 km (1,485 miles) at standard MTOW with 107 passengers and Tay 620 engines
Load: 11,242–12,147 kg (24,784–26,780 lb) with Tay 620s

A Fokker 100 of Swissair

BOEING 747 (U.S.A.)

Boeing 747-100

Known universally as the 'Jumbo Jet', the Model 747 introduced the 'wide-body' airliner concept. It is the world's largest airliner, and is the mainstay of the Western world's long-range high-capacity routes. After failing to win the U.S. Air Force's CX-HLS competition for a long-range logistic freighter, Boeing decided to capitalize on its work by developing the basic concept into a civil transport. Initial thoughts centred on a 430-seat type with a 'double bubble' fuselage configuration in which each lobe would be about 4.57m (15 ft) wide. This failed to secure major airline interest, so Boeing finally opted for a 'big brother' to the Model 707 using

basically the same layout but with a fuselage large enough to accommodate a cabin 6.13 m (20 ft 1.5 in) wide and 56.39 m (185 ft 0 in) long. The type first flew in February 1969 and, with more than 1,300 aircraft ordered, the Model 747 is still in development and production with a choice of General Electric, Pratt & Whitney and Rolls-Royce turbofan engines.

The main variants have been the initial Model 747-100 with a maximum weight of 322,051 kg (710,000 lb) and strengthened Model 747-100B, the Model 747-200 (also offered in convertible and freighter

versions) with further structural strengthening, greater fuel capacity and uprated engines for a maximum weight of 377,842 kg (833,000 lb), the Model 747SP long-range version with the fuselage reduced in length by 14.35 m (47 ft 1 in) for a maximum of 440 passengers, the Model 747SR short-range version of the Model 747-100B with features to cater for the higher frequency of take-off/landing cycles, the Model 747-300 with a

stretched upper deck increasing this area's accommodation from 16 first-class to 69 economy-class passengers, and the current Model 747-400 with structural improvements to reduce weight, a two-crew flight deck with the latest cockpit displays and instrumentation, extended wings with drag-reducing winglets on the international versions, lean-burn turbofans, and extra fuel for longer range.

BOEING 747-400

Role: Long-range passenger/cargo transport

Crew/Accommodation: Two, plus 420 passengers in a 3-class configuration or other layouts up to 568 passengers.

Power Plant: Four 26,263 kgp (57,900 lb s.t.) General Electric CF6-80C2B or 25,741 kgp (56,750 lb s.t.) Pratt & Whitney PW 4000 series or 26,308 kgp (58,000 lb s.t.) Rolls-Royce RB211-524G or higher rated H turbofans.

Dimensions: Span 64.44 m (211.4 ft); length 70.66 m (231.83 ft); wing area 520.25 m² (5,600 sq ft)

Weights: Empty 182,256 kg (402,400 lb) typically; MTOW up to 394,625 kg (870,000 lb)

Performance: Cruise speed 939 km/h (507 knots) at 10.670 m (35,000 ft); cruise altitude 12,500 m (41,000 ft); design range up to13,418 km (8,342 miles)

Load: Up to 65,230 kg (143,800 lb) with cargo

Boeing 747-400

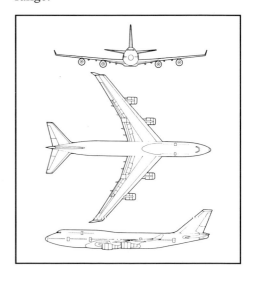

Boeing 747-400

AEROSPATIALE/BAC CONCORDE (France/United Kingdom)

Concorde

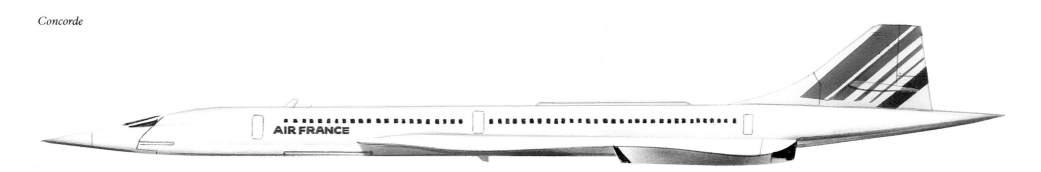

Currently the world's only supersonic air transport, the Concorde originated from separate French and British projects which were considered too expensive for single-nation development. The two efforts were therefore amalgamated in 1962 by an inter-governmental agreement. The French and British airframe contractors were Sud-Aviation and the British Aircraft Corporation, which eventually became parts of Aérospatiale and British Aerospace respectively. The project matured as a medium-sized type with a delta wing and a slender fuselage; the wing has an ogival leading edge, and the aerodynamically clean forward section of the fuselage has a 'droop snoot' arrangement to provide the crew with an adequate field of vision for take-off and landing.

The French were responsible for the wings, the rear cabin section, the flying controls, and the air-conditioning, hydraulic, navigation and radio systems; the British were tasked with the three forward fuselage sections, the rear fuselage and vertical tail, the engine nacelles and ducts, the engine installation, the electrical, fuel and oxygen systems, and the noise and thermal insulation. A similar collaborative arrangement was organized between Rolls-Royce and SNECMA for the design and construction of the engines.

The first of two prototypes, one from each country, flew in March 1969, and these two machines had slightly shorter nose and tail sections than later aircraft. The type has proved an outstanding technical success, but political and environmental opposition meant that only two pre-production and 14 production aircraft were built.

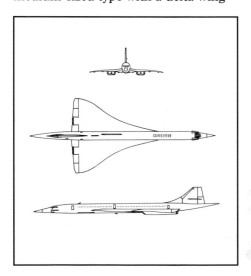

Concorde

AEROSPATIALE/BAC CONCORD
Role: Supersonic passenger transport
Crew/Accommodation: Three and four cabin crew, plus up to 144 passengers
Power Plant: Four 17,260-kgp (38,050-lb s.t.) Rolls-Royce/SNECMA Olympus 593 Mk610 turbojets with reheat
Dimensions: Span 25.6 m (84 ft): Length 67.17 m (203.96 ft); wing area 358.25 m² (3,856 sq ft)
Weights: Empty 77,110 kg (170,000 lb); MTOW 181,400 kg (400,000 lb)
Performance: Maximum speed 2,333 km/h (1,450 knots) Mach 2.05 at 16,600 m (54,500 ft); operational ceiling 18,288 m (60,000 ft); range 7,215 km (4,483 miles
Load: Typically 11,340 kg (25,000 lb)

A British Aerospace/Aerospatiale Concorde of British Airways

McDONNELL DOUGLAS and BOEING (McDONNELL DOUGLAS) MD-11 (U.S.A.)

DC-10-10

Douglas began work on the design of the DC-10 in 1966 in response to a requirement of American Airlines for a wide-body airliner offering the same sort of range as the Boeing Model 747 with a smaller payload. With orders for 55 aircraft and options for another 55 received, Douglas launched production in April 1968. The design matured as a basically conventional low-wing monoplane with swept flying surfaces, tricycle landing gear and three turbofan engines (one under each wing and the third on a vertical pylon above the rear fuselage with the vertical tail above it).

The first example flew in August 1970, by which time Douglas had amalgamated with McDonnell. A total of 386 commercial and 60 military DC-10s were ordered, the last (a KC-10A) delivered in April 1990. These included the DC-10-10 with 18,144-kg (40,000-lb thrust General Electric CF-6 turbofans for 380 passengers and which first entered service in August 1971, the DC-10-10CF convertible freight passenger transport, the DC-10-15 with 21,092-kg (46,500-lb) thrust CF6-50 engines and higher weights, the DC-10-30 intercontinental transport with the span increased by 3.05 m (10 ft 0 in), 22,226-kg (49,000-lb thrust CF6-50A/C engines, extra fuel and a two-wheel additional main landing gear unit between the standard units, the DC-10-30F freighter and DC-10-30CF convertible freighter, the DC-10-40 intercontinental version of the 30 with 22,407-kg (49,400-lb) thrust and later 24,040-kg (53,000-lb) thrust Pratt & Whitney JT9D turbofans, and 60 KC-10A Extender transport/tankers for the U.S. Air Force. The MD-11 is an updated version that first flew in January 1990. A total 192 had been ordered in airliner, freighter and combi forms, but production is expected to end in the year 2000. MD-11 features include drag-reducing winglets, on extended wings, a lengthened fuselage for up to 410 passengers, advanced avionics and a choice of modern high-thrust General Electric or Pratt & Whitney engines.

MCDONNELL DOUGLAS MD-11 airliner
Role: Long/intermediate-range passenger/cargo transport
Crew/Accommodation: Two, eight cabin crew and 250–410 passengers
Power Plant: Three 27,896 kgp (61,500 lb s.t.) General Electric CF6-80C2D1F or 27,215–28,123 kgp (60,000–62,000 lb s.t.) Pratt & Whitney PW 4460/4462 turbofans
Dimensions: Span 51.7 m (169.5 ft); length 61.62 m (202.17 ft) with G.E. engines; wing area 338.91 m² (3,648 sq ft)
Weights: Empty (operating) 130,165 kg (286,965 lb); MTOW 273,314 kg–285,990 kg (602,555–630,500 lb)
Performance: Maximum speed 946 km/h (588 mph) at 9,450 m (31,000 ft); operational ceiling 12,800 m (42,000 ft); range 12,668 km (7,871 miles) with 298 passengers, no auxillary tanks
Load: Typically 51,272 kg (113,035 lb) or up to 90,787 kg (200,151 lb) for freighter (including tare weight)

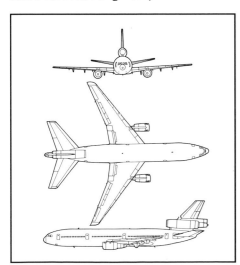

McDonnell Douglas DC-10-30

A McDonnell Douglas DC-10-30

LOCKHEED L-1011 TRISTAR (U.S.A.)

L-1011-1 TriStar

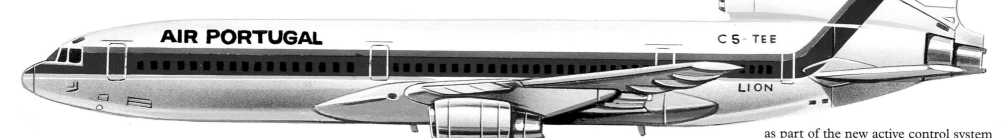

The TriStar was planned to meet an Eastern Airlines' requirement for a wide-body airliner optimized for short- and medium-range operations with a large number of passengers, and was planned in parallel with its engine, the Rolls-Royce RB.211 turbofan initially offered at a 19,051-kg (42,000-lb) thrust rating. Development problems with the engine broke Rolls-Royce and nearly broke Lockheed, both companies having to be rescued by their respective governments. Construction began in 1968, and the first TriStar flew in November 1970.

Certification was delayed until April 1972 by the two companies' financial problems, and the L-1101-1 variant entered service in the same month with RB.211-22B engines and provision for up to 400 passengers at a maximum take-off weight of 195,045-kg (430,000-lb). The L-1011-100, which was the same basic airliner with RB.211-22B engines but with the fuel capacity and weights of the L-1011-200, which first flew in 1976 with 21,772-kg (48,000-lb) thrust RB.211-524 engines and a maximum take-off weight of up to 216,363-kg (477,000-lb) depending on the fuel load. The final production model was the L-1011-500 for very long-range operations, with 22,680-kg (50,000-lb) thrust RB.211-524B engines, increased fuel capacity, the fuselage shortened by 4.11 m (13 ft 6 in) for the accommodation of between 246 and 330 passengers, and the wings increased in span by 2.74 m (9 ft 0 in)

as part of the new active control system that also saw a reduction in tailplane size. Sales failed to match Lockheed's marketing forecasts, and production ended in 1984 with the 250th aircraft. TriStars modified with the L-1011-500's engines and given a strengthened airframe and landing gear for higher gross weights (including more fuel for extended range) became L-1011-250s. Other conversions included several ex-airline aircraft converted as TriStar K.Mk 1 tankers and KC.Mk 1 tanker/freighters for the RAF.

A Lockheed L-1011-1 TriStar of Air Canada

LOCKHEED L-1011 TRISTAR
Role: Intermediate-range passenger transport
Crew/Accommodation: Three, six cabin crew, plus up to 400 passengers (charter)
Power Plant: Three 19,051 kgp (42,000 lb s.t.) Rolls-Royce RB211-22 turbofans
Dimensions: Span 47.35 m (155,33 ft); length 54.46 m (178.66 ft); wing area 321.1m² (3,456 sq ft)
Weights: Empty 106,265 kg (234,275 lb); MTOW 195,045 kg (430,000 lb)
Performance: Cruise speed 796 km/h (495 mph) at 9,140 m (30,000 ft); operational ceiling 12,800 m (42,000 ft); range 4,635 km (2,880 miles) with maximum payload
Load: Up to 41,152 kg (90,725 lb)

Lockheed TriStar K.Mk 1

AIRBUS INDUSTRIE A300 (France/Germany/Spain/U.K.)

Airbus Industrie A300 B4

The Airbus consortium was founded in 1970 to manage this European challenge to the American 'big three' of airliner production – Boeing, Lockheed and McDonnell Douglas. A number of national designs had already been studied before the consortium was created to design, develop and build a 250-seat airliner powered by two British or American turbofans. The political and economic difficulties as the programme got underway were considerable, and the two sponsoring and largest shareholding countries became France and West Germany joined by the United Kingdom and Spain that have smaller shareholdings. All became industrial participants, joined as associate members by Belgium and the Netherlands.

The first A300B1 flew in October 1972, and this was lengthened by 2.65 m (8ft 8 in) to create the basic production model, the A300B2-100 with General Electric CF6-50 engines; variants became the A300B2-200 with leading-edge flaps, the A300B2-220 with Pratt & Whitney JT9D-59A turbofans, and the A300B2-300 with higher take-off and landing weights. Then came the A300B4-100 long-range version offered with CF6 or JT91 engines, the strengthened A300B4-200 with still higher weights and the A300B4-200FF with a two-crew cockpit. The A300C4 first flew in 1979 as a convertible freighter based on the A300B4, while an all-freight model became F4. In July 1983 the first flight took place of the A300-600, the only version currently available as new, itself available in passenger, extended range (R), convertible (C) and freighter (F) variants. Total A300 sales are well over 500 aircraft

An Airbus Industrie A300-600R

AIRBUS A300-600

Role: Long/intermediate-range passenger transport

Crew/Accommodation: Two and six cabin crew plus up to 361 passengers

Power Plant: Two 25,400-kgp (56,000-lb s.t.) Pratt & Whitney PW4156 or 26,310-kgp (58,000-lb s.t.) PW4158 turbofans, or General Electric CF6-80C2As of 26,762–27,895 kgp (59,000–61,500 lb s.t.)

Dimensions: Span 44.84 m (147.1 ft); length 54.08 m (177.4 ft); wing area 260 m² (2,799 sq ft)

Weights: Empty 90,100 kg (198,636 lb); MTOW 165,000 kg (363,760 lb) typically

Performance: Maximum speed 891 km/h (554 mph) at 9,450 m (31,000 ft); operational ceiling 12,200 m (40,000 ft); range 6,852 km (4,260 miles) with G E engines and 266 passengers

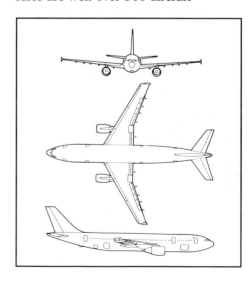

Airbus Industrie A300-600

BOEING 767 and 777 (U.S.A.)

767-200

Planned in concert with the Model 757, the Model 767 is a wide-body transport with a cabin width of 4.72 m (15.5 ft), compared with 3.53 m (11.58 ft) for the Model 757. Even so, the Models 757 and 767 have so much in common that pilots can secure a single rating for both types. Drafting was undertaken with the aid of computer-aided design techniques. The type was schemed as a high-capacity airliner for medium-range

routes, and present versions offer accommodation for 181 and 350 passengers, plus a choice of General Electric CF6-80C2B, Pratt & Whitney PW4052/4056/4060/4062, or Rolls-Royce RB211-524G4 or H turbofans. The Model 767 also differs from the Model 757 in having larger wings of increased sweep, but similar features are the tail unit, landing gear and engine pods.

The first Model 767 flew in September 1981 and, with the

cancellation of the planned Model 767-100 with a shorter fuselage for the carriage of a maximum of 180 passengers, the Model 767-200 became the basic variant, with a typical maximum take-off weight of 136,077 kg (300,000 lb) and range of 8,465 km (5,260 miles). The extended- range Model 767-200ER has additional fuel in a second centre section tank for greater range, while the Model 767-300 provides greater capacity, and has its length stretched

from 48.51 m (159.17 ft) to 54.94 m (180.25 ft). Variants include the extended range 767-300ER and 767-300F freighter. Latest version is the 767-400, launched in 1997 and offering accommodation for 303 passengers in 2-class layout and a range of 10,460 km (6,500 miles). Well over 800 767s have been ordered. The model 777 first flew in June 1994 as a long-range wide-body airliner of increased size, for up to 550 passengers

BOEING 767-300
Role: Intermediate-range passenger transport
Crew/Accommodation: Two/three, six cabin crew plus up to 290 passengers
Power Plant: Two General Electric CF6-80C2B or Pratt & Whitney PW4050/4060 series turbofans, ranging from 23,814–28,123 kgp (52,500–62,000 lb s.t.)
Dimensions: Span 47.57 m (156.08 ft); length 54.94 m (180.25 ft); wing area 283.35 m² (3,050 sq ft)
Weights: Empty 86,954 kg (191,700 lb); MTOW 159,211 kg (351,000 lb)
Performance: Maximum speed 906 km/h (563 mph) at 11,887 m (39,000 ft); operational ceiling 13,000+ m (42,650+ ft); range 6,920 km (4,300 miles)
Load: Up to 39,145 kg (86,300 lb)

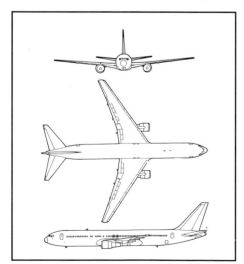

Boeing 767-300

A Boeing 767-200

BOEING 757 (U.S.A.)

Boeing 757-200

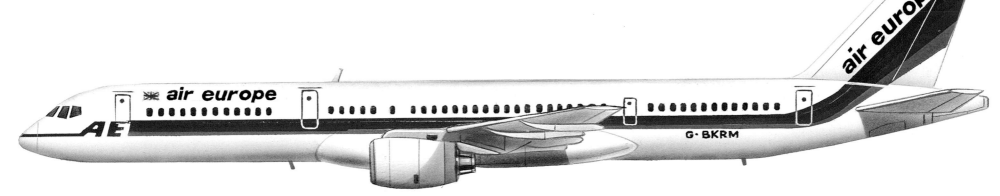

In the later part of 1978, Boeing announced its intention of developing a new generation of advanced-technology airliners. The two definitive members of this family were the Models 757 and 767, while the Model 777 was less certain. The Model 757 retained the same narrow fuselage cross-section as the Model 727, and could be regarded as the Model 727's successor in the carriage of between 150 and 239 passengers over short- and medium-range routes, while the latest 757-300 (launched 1996) can carry up to 289 persons. Where Boeing offered considerable improvement, however, was in a new standard of fuel efficiency expected to offer 45 per cent fuel savings per passenger/mile by comparison with contemporary types. The Model 757 was therefore first offered with Rolls-Royce RB211-535 or General Electric CF6-32C1 turbofans in underwing pods; General Electric then dropped the CF6-32 engine, and Pratt & Whitney entered the lists with the PW2037.

The type was originally planned in Model 757-100 short-fuselage and Model 757-200 long-fuselage variants; launch customers all opted for the latter with RB211 engines, and the shorter variant was then dropped. The Model 757-200 first flew in February 1982.

Freighter, PF Package Freighter and M combi models are also available, the PF and M each having a large main-deck cargo door. For delivery to customers from 1999, the latest 757-300 is a stretched version for 240–289 passengers, with strengthened wings and landing gear and maximum take-off weight increased to 122,470-kg (270,000-lb).

A Boeing 757-200

BOEING 757-200
Role: Intermediate-range passenger transport
Crew/Accommodation: Two, four cabin crew plus up to 239 passengers
Power Plant: Two 18,189-kgp (40,100-lb s.t.) Rolls-Royce RB211-535E4 or 17,350-kgp (38,250-lb s.t.) Pratt & Whitney PW2037 or other turbofans
Dimensions: Span 38.05 m (124.83 ft); length 47.32 m (155.25 ft); wing area 185.25 m² (1,994 sq ft)
Weights: Empty from 57,970 kg (127,800 lb); MTOW 115,666 kg (255,000 lb)
Performance: Cruise speed 950 km/h (590 mph) at 8,230 m (27,000 ft); operational ceiling 13,000+ m (42,650+ ft); range 7,278 km (4,525 miles) with PW2037 engines and maximum payload

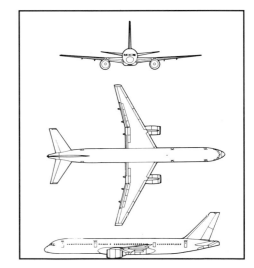

Boeing 757-200

AIRBUS INDUSTRIE A310 (France/Germany/Spain/U.K.)

Airbus Industrie A310

A major problem facing the design team of the Airbus family of airliners was the lack of clear signals from potential purchasers both in Europe and elsewhere in the world. The A310 resulted from an Airbus programme designed to produce a large-capacity airliner for the short-haul market. At one time, the programme encompassed no fewer than 11 proposals designed to attract the widest possible spectrum of potential buyers. The final A310 was designed to satisfy the emerging market for a 200-seater offering the same type of fuel economy as the A300, and was indeed designed for the highest possible commonality with the A300. Thus the A310 may be regarded as a short-fuselage derivative of the A300, with other features including aerodynamically clean outer wing areas without vortex generators, offering a lift coefficient usefully higher than that of the A300.

The type was first flown in April 1982, entering service in 1983. It was proposed in A310-100 short-range and A310-200 medium-range versions, but the former was dropped in favour of different-weight versions of the A310-200 optimized for the two roles. The A310-300 is a longer range version with drag-reducing wingtip fences (retrospectively applied to the A310-200) and a tailplane trim tank, available in the weight options for the A310-200. Convertible and freight versions are designated A310C and A310F.

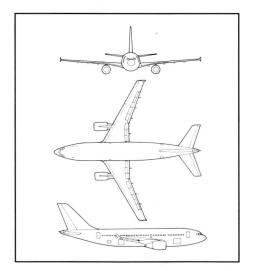

Airbus Industrie A310

AIRBUS A310-300
Role: Intermediate-range passenger transport
Crew/Accommodation: Two flight and six cabin crew, plus up to 280 passengers
Power Plant: Two 23,586-kgp (52,000-lb s.t.) Pratt & Whitney PW4152 or 4156A or 24,267-kgp (53,500-lb s.t.) General Electric CF6-80C2A2 or more powerful CF6-80C2A8 turbofans
Dimensions: Span 43.9 m (144.0 ft); length 44.66 m (153.08 ft); wing area 219 m² (2,357 sq ft)
Weights: Empty 80,800 kg (178,113 lb); MTOW 164,000 kg (361,558 lb)
Performance: Maximum speed 903 km/h (561 mph) at 10,670 m (35,000 ft); operational ceiling 13,000+ m (42,650 ft); range up to 9,630 km (5,988 miles) with P & W engines and 220 passengers
Load: Maximum for A310C is 41,500 kg (91,490 lb), structural

An Airbus Industrie A310-300

AIRBUS INDUSTRIE A340 (France/Germany/Spain/U.K.)

Airbus Industrie A340-300

The A340 was launched as a project on 5 June 1987. At the time it was the largest aircraft to achieve production status in Europe. A340-200 is the reduced capacity version with a length of 59.39 m (194.83 ft), while the A340-300 is the standard length model for up to 440 passengers. Singapore Airlines was the first operator (in 1996) to receive an ultra-long-range and higher weight A340-300E. Further versions are the A340-400E as a variant of A340-300 but with a 6.4m (21.0 ft) fuselage stretch and CFM56-5C4 engines, the A340-500 short-fuselage and longer-range variant of the A340-600 with engine options including Rolls-Royce Trents, the stretched A340-600 with more engine power for 378 passengers in 3-class layout (enlarged and improved wings), and the proposed A340-800 for up to 400 passengers (MTOW 275,000 kg/606,270 lb). First flight of the -200 was October 1991.

First customer for the A340 was Lufthansa, as a replacement for DC-10s and entering service in March 1993.

In June 1993 the A340-200 prototype set several international distance records in its class by flying non-stop from Paris to New Zealand.

Another first for the A340 series was their being fitted with toilet facilities especially for handicapped passengers, plus a collapsible wheelchair for in-flight use.

The Airbus A330 is a twin-engined variant, first flown in November 1992 and corresponds in size to the A340-300.

Airbus Industrie A340-300

AIRBUS A340-300
Role: Long-range passenger transport
Crew/Accommodation: Two pilots and cabin crew plus up to 440 passengers
Power Plant: Four 14,152-kgp (31,200-lb s.t.) CFM International CFM56-5C2 turbofans initially, with 14,742 kgp (32,500 lb s.t.), -5C3 and 15,442 kgp (34,000lb s.t.), -5C4s optional
Dimensions: Span 60.3 m (197.83 ft); length 63.69 m (208.92 ft); wing area 363.1 m² (3,908.37 sq ft)
Weights: Empty 126,870 kg (279,700 lb); MTOW 257,000 kg (566,587 lb)
Performance: Cruise speed 890 km/h (553 mph); range 12,225 km (7,600 miles); operational ceiling 12,200m (40,000 ft);
Load: About 47,690 kg (105,139 lb)

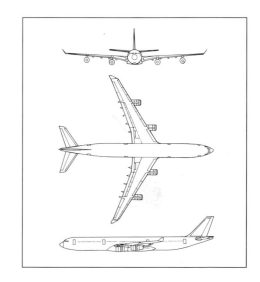

Airbus Industrie A340-300

Airbus A330 is the twin-engined variant of A340-300, with similar advanced aerofoil sections, high-lift devices, extended fly-by-wire and computer flight control system, and more

SATIC A300-600ST SUPER TRANSPORTER 'BELUGA' (France/Germany)

SATIC A300-600ST 'Beluga'

From 1971, the Airbus Industrie Consortium transported major assemblies of aircraft sections between their various manufacturing and assembly plants using a fleet of four converted Boeing Stratocruisers. These, known as 'Super Guppies', had proved successful but were in need of replacement. They were finally retired in October 1997.

There being no suitable replacement available with a huge open fuselage cross-section for outsized cargo, the consortium developed its own outsize transporter.

The result is the SATIC A300-600ST 'Beluga' Airbus Super Transporter which flew for the first time on 13 September 1994. SATIC (Special Aircraft Transport International Company) was formed jointly by Deutsche Aerospace Airbus and Aérospatiale in 1991 to build the aircraft. The 600ST has 80 per cent of spares in common with the basic aircraft, the A300-600R Airbus, with corresponding low maintenance costs.

The design employs five major conversions or modifications over the original A300 airframe. These are: an increase from 5.3 m (17.4 ft) to 7.4 m (24.3 ft) in the fuselage diameter, the lowering of the cockpit to below and forward of the freight floor level, reinforcement of the cargo floor, installation of an upper deck cargo door, and the redesigning and reinforcement of the tail plane surfaces.

The cockpit layout is identical to the A300-600R. Payloads are inserted through the main forward freight door, the largest ever fitted to an aircraft, which opens upwards above the cockpit. The aircraft can be loaded or unloaded by two men within 45 minutes turn-round schedule, compared with two hours, by 8 to 10 men for the Super Guppy. Maximum payload has increased to 45.5 tonnes, held in a cargo compartment of 1,400 cubic metres volume.

Four Belugas had been delivered by 1998, with the fifth and last expected in 2001.

Airbus became aware that other industries could require 'super transport' availability, including the European Space Agency, and in 1996 Airbus Transport International was formed to offer charter services using any spare Beluga capacity from the main Airbus activities.

The first SATIC A300-600ST 'Beluga' (still in primer) takes off for its maiden flight 13 September 1994

SATIC A300-600ST 'BELUGA'
Role: Heavy lift freighter
Crew/Accommodation: Pilot and co-pilot plus 2 handlers with folding seats in the cockpit
Power Plant: Two 26,762-kgp (59,000- lb s.t.) General Electric CF-6-80C2A8 turbofans
Dimensions: Span 44.84 m (147.083 ft); length 56.16 m (184.25 ft); wing area 260 m² (2,798.6 sq ft)
Weights: MTOW 150,000 kg (330,693 lb)
Performance: Cruise speed 778 km/h (484 mph); range 1,666 km (1,035 miles)
Load: Up to 45,500 kg (100,310 lb)

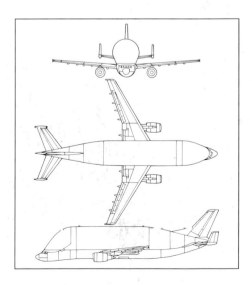

SATIC A300-600ST 'Beluga'